HORRORS OF HISTORY

OCEAN OF FIRE

T. NEILL ANDERSON

imi Charlesbridge

MTM Publishing, Inc.
435 West 23rd Street, #8C
New York, NY 10011
www.mtmpublishing.com

President: Valerie Tomaselli
Series creator: Hilary Poole
Designer: Annemarie Redmond
Illustrator: Richard Garratt
Copyeditor: Sandra Smith
Academic advisor: Jacqueline Glass Campbell

Published by Charlesbridge
85 Main Street
Watertown, MA 02472
(617) 926-0329
www.charlesbridge.com

Library of Congress Cataloging-in-Publication Data
Anderson, T. Neill.
Horrors of history: ocean of fire / T. Neill Anderson.
p. cm
Summary: While her father and uncle, chemists at South Carolina College, try to get scientific
equipment to safety, seventeen-year-old Emma hides with the rest of her family and
others in their basement as Confederate soldiers bomb and loot Columbia.
ISBN 978-1-58089-516-3 (reinforced for library use)
ISBN 978-1-60734-541-1 (ebook)
ISBN 978-1-60734-621-0 (ebook pdf)
1. Columbia (S.C.)—History—Burning, 1865—Juvenile fiction. [1. Columbia (S.C.)—
History—Burning, 1865—Fiction. 2. Survival—Fiction. 3. Refugees—Fiction. 4. Slavery—
Fiction. 5. Family life—South Carolina—Fiction. 6. United States—History—Civil
War, 1861–1865—Fiction.] I. Title. II. Title: Ocean of fire.
PZ7.A5516Chr 2014
[Fic]—dc23   2013004291

Printed in China
(hc) 10 9 8 7 6 5 4 3 2 1

Display type set in Cracked and text type set in Adobe Caslon Pro
Printed and bound September 2013
by Jade Productions in Heyuan, Guangdong, China

TABLE OF CONTENTS

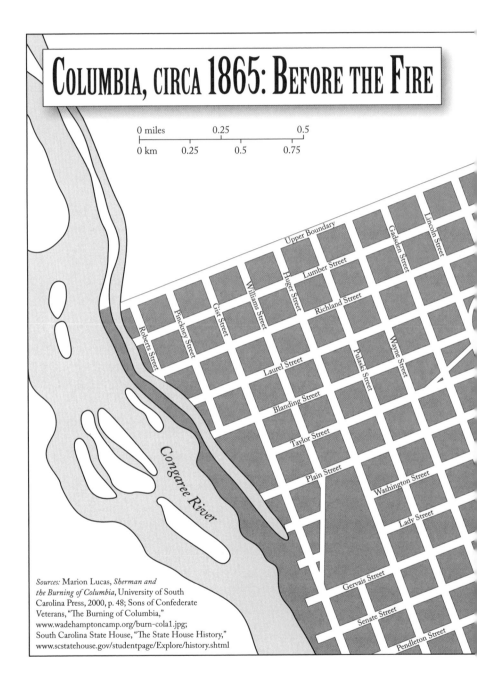

Columbia, circa 1865: Before the Fire

0 miles   0.25   0.5

0 km   0.25   0.5   0.75

Upper Boundary

Gadsden Street

Lincoln Street

Lumber Street

Huger Street

Williams Street

Richland Street

Gist Street

Pinckney Street

Roberts Street

Wayne Street

Laurel Street

Pulaski Street

Blanding Street

Taylor Street

Plain Street

Congaree River

Washington Street

Lady Street

Gervais Street

Senate Street

Pendleton Street

Sources: Marion Lucas, *Sherman and the Burning of Columbia,* University of South Carolina Press, 2000, p. 48; Sons of Confederate Veterans, "The Burning of Columbia," www.wadehamptoncamp.org/burn-cola1.jpg; South Carolina State House, "The State House History," www.scstatehouse.gov/studentpage/Explore/history.shtml

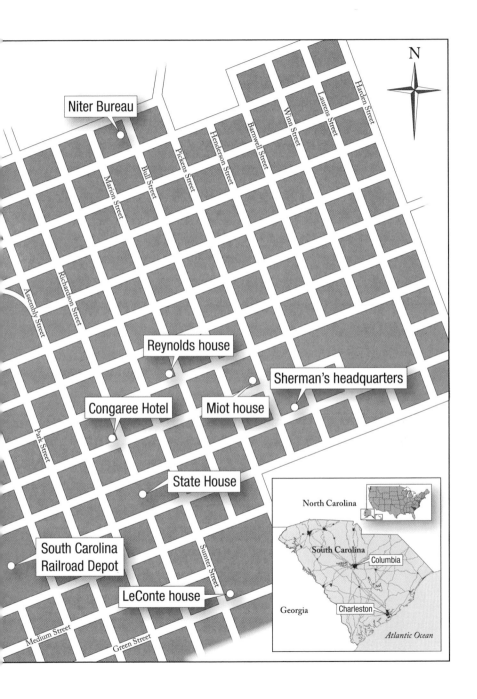

Niter Bureau

Harden Street

Laurens Street

Winn Street

Barnwel Street

Henderson Street

Pickens Street

Bull Street

Marion Street

Richardson Street

Assembly Street

Reynolds house

Sherman's headquarters

Congaree Hotel

Miot house

Park Street

State House

South Carolina
Railroad Depot

Sumter Street

LeConte house

Medium Street

Green Street

N

North Carolina

South Carolina

Columbia

Georgia

Charleston

Atlantic Ocean

*It was about four o'clock and the State House
was one grand conflagration. Imagine night turned into
noonday, only with a blazing, scorching glare that was
horrible—a copper colored sky across which swept columns of
black, rolling smoke glittering with sparks and flying embers,
while all around us were falling thickly showers of burning
flakes. Everywhere the palpitating blaze walling the streets
with solid masses of flames as far as the eye could reach, filling
the air with its horrible roar. On every side the crackling and
devouring fire, while every instant came the crashing of
timbers and the thunder of falling buildings.*

—Emma LeConte, February 18, 1865
When the World Ended: The Diary of Emma LeConte

PROLOGUE

Columbia, South Carolina
February 15, 1865

THE SOUTH CAROLINA RAILROAD DEPOT overflowed with terrified would-be passengers and desperate cries for help. The train whistle shrieked, indicating the overcrowded locomotive was about to leave for Richmond. Panicked women begged to be let on the train as conductors shook their heads—"Sorry, no room"—and soldiers stood by to keep what peace remained. Some mothers smashed windows, then lifted up and pushed their children into the train cars, headfirst, feetfirst, whichever way they could.

A drizzle cloaked the dusky sky as a mass of terrified women and red-faced children rushed the train, drawn to it like metal shavings to a magnet. But the train was filled to suffocation, and the attendants pushed the weeping women away.

"Don't know why there's so much fuss. . . ." A bored depot attendant leaned against a ticket counter, reading a newspaper. But even as he spoke, the booming of Yankee artillery sounded louder in the distance. The headline on the front page of the newspaper read, "City Officials: Columbia Cotton to Be Burned."

A woman who had just been turned away from the train shouted at him. "Sherman's men are on the other side of the river!"

The attendant nodded. "Word has it they are on their way here from Charleston." He shrugged at the panicked woman. "Don't you fret, ma'am, our boys'll defend Columbia."

"Well, they better!" she spat.

He smiled. "Oh, they'll be here."

Steam rose around the train as it pulled away from the station, on its way now to the Confederate capital. Women ran after it waving and wailing, pulling their confused children behind them. But the train moved on, deaf to their cries.

Soon the last remnants of daylight were gone, but the night was no quieter than the day, as the sounds of agitated citizens, train whistles, and cannon fire filled the air. In the restless dark, a wagon train moved along, passing street after street filled with bales of cotton stacked high. The wagons rumbled softly, as if they were afraid of being noticed.

It was a Confederate army train, half a mile long and full of soldiers stealing away in the night and leaving Columbia to its doom.

Columbia Will Fall

A CANNON'S DISTANT BOOM JOLTED seventeen-year-old Emma LeConte where she sat, sending her embroidery needle into her index finger. She bit her lip so as not to scream and sucked the blood off her finger. She stood up, walked out on the porch of her family's house on the campus of South Carolina College, and heard the wagons rattling briskly down the streets on their way out of town. Looking out beyond the campus gate, she saw black smoke from the firing cannons and listened to the cacophony in the air: shrieking train whistles, women shouting in the streets, and children yelping, simultaneously excited and frightened. She stretched out her hand—the rain had finally stopped.

From where she stood on the porch, she heard her baby sister wailing downstairs. She walked inside and padded down to the basement, where Carrie was lying in a basket on the floor. Emma and her mother, Bessie, had been sleeping down there by the fire for the past few weeks so they could keep an eye on Carrie, who had been sick with the measles. Emma's sister Sallie spent most of her time these days holed up in her room, pacing

Sketch of Sherman's troops burning McPhersonville, Georgia, by William Ward, 1865. Columbia residents feared their city would be next.

back and forth, jabbering to herself in terror of the Yankee invasion she was sure was coming any second.

Emma, for her part, wasn't very frightened—she'd gotten used to doomsday talk. The threat of annihilation by the Yankees, whom South Carolinians called "Sherman's hellhounds," was usual talk in the streets these days. This war had begun when she was thirteen, and now, four years later, she could hardly remember a time when victory over the Yankees wasn't what she craved every hour of every day. If the rumors were to be believed, the war was coming to Columbia: Sherman and his army of sixty thousand loathsome Yankees had burned Atlanta and other Georgia towns and cut a path all the way to Savannah, and now they were heading to South Carolina, the "cradle" of secession. Rumors abounded in Columbia that Sherman had handled Georgia with gloves on but that, in South Carolina, he would take them off.

Over the past few weeks, she'd heard it all: the city would be burned to cinders, every home would be sacked and destroyed, Columbia would be brought to its very knees as punishment for its role in fanning the flames of the conflict. As Emma had written in her diary, "They are preparing to hurl destruction upon the State they hate most of all, and Sherman the brute avows his intention of converting South Carolina into a wilderness. How we hate them with the whole strength and depth of our souls!"

But then her own uncle John had asserted that England and France would recognize the Confederacy as a separate nation in just a few weeks—certainly by the first week in March—which would surely help the Southern cause. A few days ago rumors flew that Sherman would not come to Columbia after all. Many Columbians were still hopeful for a negotiated peace with the Yankees. Just yesterday Mayor Goodwyn had announced that the highest military authorities had assured him that Columbia was safe. But Emma knew how many times they had been puffed up with false hope, only to be disappointed over and over.

Then, yesterday, an intense excitement filled the streets as the Yankees were reported just a few miles off on the other side of the Congaree River. But after months of the most awful speculation about Columbia's fate, Emma just couldn't bring herself to surrender to fright today. That Columbia might suffer the same fiery fate as Atlanta was too horrible even to contemplate.

In any event, Emma was determined that her family would not give up in this fight, absolutely not. She, Sallie, and Bessie would protect their house and their possessions as fiercely as possible with the help of Henry, Mary Ann, and their other slaves. The way Emma saw it, to show fear was to hand the Yankees a small victory before they even arrived. Sherman's hellhounds deserved no such courtesy.

But just because she wasn't ready to believe the worst didn't mean she wasn't taking precautions. Like many girls her age, Emma had a substantial collection of letters and diaries that she treasured above all her other possessions. She dreaded the thought of her papers sharing the same fate as those of her aunt Jane and her cousin Ada, who'd been driven from their homes in Liberty County, Georgia. Their letters were rifled through—probably read in full—and scattered along the roads, offered up to anyone whose nosiness exceeded their good sense. Emma had spent the last hour destroying most of her letters, but there were some that she couldn't bring herself to burn. If the Yankees did indeed do their worst to Columbia, these few letters might be the only record she would have of her previous life. What to do with them? Perhaps she could bury them in the yard. But then she pictured brutish soldiers digging them up and tossing them to the wind.

Emma decided that the only way to keep her letters secure was to keep them with her at all times. So she'd sewed several large pockets that she could fill with her most precious possessions and then, when the moment came, tie under her hoopskirt. As long as she was able to stand against the invaders, her letters would be safe.

After rocking Carrie back to sleep, she hurried up to her bedroom, where she sat on her bed packing the pockets she'd made with treasures from her little jewelry box. Suddenly a new commotion from outside reached her ears. Peering out her window into the darkness, she could see the ambulance wagons bringing in wounded soldiers to the buildings near her house on the campus, which had been converted into hospital facilities for both Confederate and Yankee soldiers wounded in various campaigns. Beaten and bloody men were pulled from the wagons and carried inside, their moans of pain filling her ears and quickening her heartbeat. She then shifted her gaze to the stranger carrying a lantern and approaching her house with a dark and determined look on his face.

A young soldier in Confederate gray slowly approached the LeConte house. But when he reached the porch, instead of knocking, he stopped and lit a cigarette. Walking toward him was Joseph LeConte, Emma's father, who was finally arriving home from the train depot. He had been there to check that his laboratory boxes, which the Confederate capital at Richmond had instructed him to pack up and send away, had successfully made it on board the train. As the official chemist overseeing the Confederate government's manufacturing of medicines and chemicals such as chloroform, alcohol, and nitrate of silver, Joseph's job was to ensure that all these chemicals were safe from the enemy. Now most of them were on their way by train to Richmond. LeConte was also responsible for the potassium nitrate used to make gunpowder, currently stored at the Niter and Mining Bureau in the northern part of town. LeConte would have to ensure that the chemicals were safe from the approaching enemy. But he would make a short stop at home first.

Joseph was surprised to see the soldier standing at the porch, waiting for him, as if the young man knew precisely what time Joseph would be returning.

"Dr. LeConte," the soldier said with a nervous smile, "I'm very happy to have caught you. Been anxious to talk."

Joseph LeConte, circa 1874

"Great God, it's a surprise to see you, Davis!" Joseph said, shaking Davis's hand. "Please, let's go inside." He wondered aloud how Davis had found his house.

"Oh, Dr. LeConte, you know I have my ways of finding things out," Davis said with a wink.

Joseph's shock at finding Davis at his doorstep was evident. He had met Davis just a few weeks earlier, during the last leg of a harrowing trip he'd undertaken through war-torn Georgia. Since General Sherman had left Atlanta and begun his already infamous "march to the sea," Joseph feared for the safety of his widowed sister Jane, his two nieces Ada and Annie, and his daughter Sallie, who were all staying at the family plantation at Halifax, thirty-five miles south of Savannah. Joseph had embarked on a difficult journey across enemy lines in the dead of winter to bring them back. They went without food for days while hiding from enemy soldiers before reaching the family plantation in Liberty—only to find that their home had been completely plundered by the Federal army. It took them five weeks to get back to Columbia.

They were on the tail end of their return trip when they met up with a mysterious young man in Confederate gray going by the name of Charles Davis. They had been rushing to catch a train at the Macon depot, and as their wagon approached, Joseph could see the train cars slowly pulling away.

"Quick!" he'd shouted at their driver. "Quick, that's our train leaving!" Joseph leaped out of the wagon in a panic—getting left behind in Macon was an unwelcome thought to say the least. He helped the women out of the wagon and struggled with the bountiful luggage, while the women tried to get the conductor's attention. Seeing their predicament from the window, Davis ran to the conductor to have him stop the train, then helped the ladies aboard while Joseph handled the bags.

Davis traveled with them until they reached Augusta, regaling the LeContes with his tales of horrific battles and narrow escapes during the Georgia campaign. He would point out places of desperate and bloody conflict. "Yonder, under that tree, I killed a Yankee in self-defense," he would say, or "Over on that ridge I barely escaped with my life." But there was something curious about this man. He said he was twenty years old and a member of Colonel Joseph Lewis's Kentucky cavalry brigade.

He was well spoken, good-looking, and quick-witted, yet he was cloaked in mystery. He could be candid and talkative at one moment and strangely evasive the next. Joseph's nieces didn't know what to make of him.

"He's very handsome and charming," Ada said, "but. . . ." She shrugged.

Davis told Joseph that he was a Confederate spy, and the fact that he knew all about Sherman's army—the numbers of every corps and division, down to the minutest detail, as well as the names and personal characteristics of all the officers—certainly supported this claim.

"I wouldn't be surprised at all if he was, in fact, a *Yankee* spy," Joseph's sister Jane had whispered, only half-joking. Because, indeed, Davis's knowledge of Sherman's army also pointed to this possibility.

Joseph didn't know what to make of Davis. His assistance on the trip was selfless and admirable, but Joseph wasn't completely sure if he could trust him.

In saying good-bye to the LeContes in Augusta, Davis had shaken Joseph's hand and then said to the group, "I shall soon see you again in Columbia. The Yankees are certainly going there, and I shall be wherever they are."

Joseph soon forgot about Mr. Davis, burdened as he was with getting his family back home. But now here was this mysterious stranger once again, clad in Confederate gray and looking exceedingly uneasy.

"Dr. LeConte, it is terribly important that you and your family leave Columbia at once," Davis said in a low voice as they entered the house and moved into the back parlor. "The Yankees will likely arrive in the city tomorrow."

Nearby, Mary Ann, one of the domestic slaves, crouched on the other side of the kitchen door. She listened to Davis's words with her hand over her mouth and her eyes wide with fear.

"I've been in the Yankee camp all day," Davis continued, "and I know all their plans."

Joseph asked, "What will happen to Columbia if it is taken by the Yankees?"

Davis was silent for a few moments before answering. "I fear to tell you what scenes will be enacted in Columbia, Dr. LeConte."

"Mr. Davis . . ."

Unidentified soldier dressed in a South Carolina Confederate uniform—what Mr. Davis would have worn

"I do think, however, that I can save your house as well as your brother John's house. I believe it's on the north side of campus, on Pendleton?"

"Yes, yes, that's John's house. How did you . . ."

"I've managed to gain some influence with Yankee officers," Davis continued. He rubbed his thumb and fingers together to indicate that the influence was purchased. "I'd be happy to give you letters of protection to present to Yankee colonels, to ensure your family's safety once you're on the road." He reached into his coat to retrieve a pen.

"Thank you, Mr. Davis, for the kind offer, but I'd rather not be caught up in such intrigue."

"Sir, surely you don't doubt that the Yankees' arrival is imminent?"

"No, I don't doubt that. Though I've been assured that Hardee's corps are on their way from Charleston."

"Sherman's men will be here first." Joseph was silent, so Davis continued. "Would a horse help facilitate your exit? I'm sure I can secure you one."

"No, no, that won't be necessary; we have horses available to us at the college."

"Well then," Davis said, his face full of worry, "I'll check back later tonight and bring you any news I'll have. I do hope you will prepare yourselves to leave this house. Staying can only bring sorrow."

The men shook hands and walked to the front door. Davis, seeing Emma coming down the stairs, leaned in and said to Joseph, "If Yankees do enter your house, you must not look surprised to see me among them. If you recognize me, don't betray me."

"Evening, ma'am." Mr. Davis nodded to Emma as he turned and opened the front door.

Emma had been listening to the hushed conversation from the top of the stairs, and she had noticed Davis's extreme disquiet. Seeing the look on his face, she felt a pang of anxiety.

Hadn't General Hampton proclaimed just yesterday that Sherman would not come to Columbia?

She and Joseph watched Davis amble away from the house and disappear into the darkness.

"Father, what does this man know?" she asked. "Can he really have more information than the generals?"

Mary Ann rushed over to the stove and began scrubbing furiously. Joseph's conversation with the stranger played and replayed in her mind. Could it be true that the Yankees would take Columbia? After she finished cleaning the kitchen, she darted out toward the slave quarters in the backyard, where her husband, Henry, was chopping wood.

"Henry! Henry," she whispered.

Henry looked up mid-swing and held the ax over his head briefly before bringing it down to the ground with a huff and leaning on the handle.

"Woman, you know not to mess with me when I got this ax in my hand, now."

"I'm sorry, sweet, but I just overheard something you'll wanna hear."

"Well, what is it?"

"Yankees gonna be here tomorrow. In the morning."

At this news Henry released the ax, letting it fall to the ground, and sunk down onto the tree stump behind him, his tired face suddenly thoughtful.

"Who say that?"

"Some butternut was in the parlor, talking to Master Joseph."

"How do he know?"

"He was with the Yankees earlier."

Henry furrowed his brow. "Why?"

"Lord, I don't know," Mary Ann said, shaking her head. "He just was."

Henry stood. "Well, best get this wood inside and down the basement."

"Henry." Mary Ann stopped him as he began gathering the logs. "What you think we gonna have to do when they come?"

"Lord knows. Shine their boots, fix 'em food, dance for 'em."

"No, fool," Mary Ann said as Henry turned to go into the house. "I mean . . . we gonna leave?"

"Ain't convinced we should." Henry turned back around, his arms loaded with firewood. "Them Yankees may be fightin' for us, but they ain't our friends. You know that."

Mary Ann was silent. There had been rumors coming from Georgia and the low country that slave quarters had been plundered and pillaged just as badly as the masters' houses had, sometimes worse. And there had been terrifying stories of slave women being brutally attacked and raped. Even killed. Were these stories true?

With a chill down her back, she realized they might find out by tomorrow.

＊＊＊

At the Columbia home of Dr. William Reynolds, Magdalen Porter sat at the sitting room window, nervously tapping her finger against the glass. Playful hollering erupted from the hallway as her two-year-old daughter, Anna, dashed into the room to escape her brother, Theodore, nine, who was chasing her with a pillowcase on his head and growling like a monster.

"Theodore! Take that off and put it back where you found it!" Magdalen scolded. "That's not yours—we are guests in this house, and we're going to behave like it."

"Aw, Mama," Theodore said as he pulled off the pillowcase. He slunk back down the hall, and Anna, after quietly clinging to her mother's skirt for a few more moments, hurried after him.

Turning back to the window, Magdalen clapped her hands with excitement at what she saw. She flung open the front door and rushed out to meet her husband, the Reverend Anthony T. Porter, who was arriving back from a short trip to Charleston, which they'd recently fled.

"Oh, I've been so worried, dear heart!" she exclaimed, taking the box out of his arms and putting it down on the porch. "This town is in an absolute panic!"

"Yes." Porter hugged his wife. "The train station is heaving with poor souls desperately trying to get out."

"And Charleston?" She bit her lip, knowing one of the things her husband had planned to do while he was there.

"It's already a defeated city. The last service at the church was filled with sunken, tired people." He paused, collecting his thoughts. "I did visit young Toomer." Magdalen nodded with wet eyes. Their eleven-year-old son had died of yellow fever not long ago. It had been terribly painful for Magdalen to flee Charleston and leave her boy so recently buried there.

"Magnolia Cemetery . . . ," he began, his voice trailing off. "We'll remove him to our plot in Georgetown after the blockade

Charleston in ruins, documented by photographer Mathew Brady

is over." He squeezed his wife's hand, and she dabbed her eyes with a handkerchief. Changing the subject, he said, "I met with General Hardee as well. He said that Sherman has left Savannah and is moving into South Carolina and will soon be in Charleston. He told me, 'Unless you're prepared to take the oath of allegiance to the US government, you should leave Charleston.' I told him that I would take that oath when the flag of the Confederacy is folded up, but not until then."

Magdalen gave a worried smile as a delighted shriek erupted from inside the house. Little Anna came running out onto the porch, squealing wildly as her brother chased after her, hunched over like an ogre and laughing. Anna ran smack into her mother, hiding herself under Magdalen's hoop skirt.

"Yes," Reverend Porter repeated, laughing, "not until then."

———⋯———

After supper, Joseph LeConte walked to his brother John's house on the north side of campus, the booming of artillery sounding in the air to the west. He passed the ambulance wagons unloading more wounded soldiers, and the sight made him glad that night had fallen. If it had been daylight, he would have seen that the grass he walked on was stained crimson. Of course, he knew it was there—blood, pus, clumps of hair, and fragments of bone. But nightfall shrouded these grim artifacts in darkness, allowing him to walk by, knowing but not seeing. He tipped his hat to some of the ambulance crew standing by the wagon as he passed.

He wondered if John had received any further news from either the generals or the capitol at Richmond. His brother was also a chemist at the college and was superintendent of the works of the Niter Bureau, whose headquarters was on the northern outskirts of town. As he approached John's house, he saw John's wife, Josie, through the window, offering someone a beverage from a tray. He stepped up, rapped on the door, and went inside.

A thick dread filled the dimly lit room. John was perched in his regular reading chair, and sitting on the couch, sipping a cup of hot tea, was Captain Allen J. Green, a refined gentleman with a well-kept beard and a perpetually forlorn expression. This night Green, of the commanding post at Columbia, looked even more ill at ease than usual.

"Joseph," John said, skipping any formalities, "we need to depart. At once."

"For God's sake," Joseph sighed, "with every minute that passes, the night becomes darker."

"It's quite plain," began Captain Green, "that Columbia will fall. The authorities have finally confessed that we cannot hold the city."

"So Hardee will not come," Joseph said.

"And no one knows where Stuart and Cheatham are," Green quickly replied. "Their corps of roughly six thousand were expected here days ago."

Davis's words echoed now in Joseph's head: *It is terribly important that you and your family leave Columbia at once.*

"I've been instructed," Green continued, "to leave as soon as possible with whatever Niter Bureau supplies I can take with me."

"It is likely, Joseph," John said, "that if we stay, the Yankees will take us prisoner. In fact, our positions as Confederate officers make this a near certainty."

Joseph sighed. "So we must leave. But we are targets—the women must stay."

"Protected, of course," Captain Green said. "We'll leave them with letters to give to invading officers."

"That the houses are so close to the hospital will likely work in our favor," John said.

"John, you remember Mr. Davis, the odd soldier I told you about?" Joseph asked. His brother nodded. "He turned up at the house tonight."

"Really? How did he find you?"

"Oh, there's no getting easy answers out of that one," Joseph said, shaking his head. "But he urged us to go and has vowed to protect our houses."

"And you trust that he will?"

Joseph hesitated but then nodded. "Under the circumstances, I suppose I have to."

"So!" Green said, "We must pack everything we can. It is our solemn duty to save what government property is in our care. You gentlemen will want to pack your offices—all of your lecture notes, manuscripts, and the like. And any valuables from your homes, of course. Mustn't leave any toys for those damned Yankees to play with. We can send all of it up to the bureau to take with us."

"We'd better get started," John said. "We'll bring young Johnnie with us to help."

"John, it's not a bad idea to have another pair of strong arms with us," Joseph said, "but is he well enough yet? To travel under such . . . severe circumstances?"

"Still coughing a bit," John replied. "Measles'll do that to you. But they can't keep a young boy down. Fifteen he is now! And ready to be out of the house, I'd say." He chuckled. "He wouldn't dream of being left at home with the women."

"So, we'll meet at Joseph's house in two hours to finish loading up the wagon, then we'll make the walk up to the bureau behind it," Green interjected. "Time is of the essence. Say your good-byes, gentlemen, and steel yourselves for a joyless journey."

The LeContes spent the next couple of hours packing all of their clothing and bedding, as well as the family silver and jewelry, into boxes to be sent away. They left only the clothes on their backs, a change of underclothing, and blankets to sleep on. Joseph packed away his manuscripts, unpublished works, and lecture notes, and he and his slaves loaded up a wagon.

Emma handed Carrie over to her father, and Joseph covered the crying baby's wet face with kisses. Emma stood back as her father hugged and kissed her stone-faced mother and a nearly hysterical Sallie and said good-bye to his sister-in-law, Josie. He then stepped over to Emma and hugged her tightly.

"Take care of your mother and sisters, Emma," he whispered into her ear. "I worry their fears may get the best of them."

"Of course, Father," Emma said, giving him a kiss on the cheek. "I'd recruit Aunt Josie to that task as well, but she seems to be in the same state as Sallie."

"As you know, Mr. Davis has promised protection for our houses," Joseph said softly. He looked at Bessie, who had scooped up Carrie and was rocking back and forth as she said good-bye to John. "He's helped us before, of course, so I think we can take him at his word. Still, use caution in your dealings with him, Emma."

Emma nodded. The entire LeConte family stood on their porch with Captain and Mrs. Green. They watched as the wagon carrying their most valuable possessions headed north on Sumter Street toward the Niter Bureau. Joseph looked over at Josie, who was fidgeting nervously as she watched John say good-bye to Bessie and Sallie. His eyes then landed on the figure of Mr. Davis, who was walking slowly up to the house and smiling brightly at the sight of the packed wagon. He politely waited for the hugging and kissing to stop before announcing himself.

"Mr. Davis, thank you for stopping in," Joseph said. "As you can see, I've taken your advice—well, partially."

"How partially?" Davis asked.

"Well, John and I are heading to Athens to deliver the bureau supplies—we're under orders to do so immediately. But we feel the roads are too dangerous for the women and children. So Bessie and the girls will be staying. We've packed all of our valuables to take with us. I trust I can rely on your protection of our houses when the armies enter."

"Absolutely," Davis said. "I myself will make sure that no harm comes to your families."

Hearing these assurances, Emma couldn't help but think about the words she'd heard Davis utter earlier while talking to Joseph in the parlor: *I fear to tell you what scenes will be enacted in Columbia.* How was he so sure he could keep them from harm if such an unspeakable Yankee nightmare approached?

The men were soon on their way, walking the distance to the Niter Bureau, with six slaves trailing the loaded-up wagon on foot.

Sallie took Carrie inside, and Bessie followed her, her arm around a weeping Josie.

Emma remained on the porch, looking at Davis, who was still gazing at the retreating wagon. Father had advised her to be wary of Davis, but . . . she needed to know what he knew. And there was only one way to find out.

"Mr. Davis, would you like to come in for a cup of tea?"

WAILING AND WRITHING

IN THE EARLY MORNING LIGHT, a small caravan of five wagons crawled along the road. Four white men and twenty-two black men made up its entourage. Joseph, John, young Johnnie, and Captain Green strode alongside the vehicles, as did the six slaves from the LeConte households in Columbia and five slave workers from the bureau. The slaves had begged the LeConte brothers to allow their families to go with them, and after much cajoling, the women and children were allowed to ride in the wagons.

"This is a sad burden," John said to Joseph as they walked in the open air. "I wish we could have said no. These poor women and children are just extra mouths for us to feed. And extra weight to carry up these steep hillsides. We'll have to cross the swamp pretty soon, and there's no telling where the Yankees'll be hiding."

"Well, we just couldn't refuse them," Joseph said. "Their men volunteered to take the trip with us. I didn't have it in me to say no to women with crying children in their arms."

"They're gonna slow us down, Uncle Joe," young Johnnie added. His voice was hoarse from the coughing fits he'd had all night. "What happens if we need to outrun some bloody bluecoats?"

Joseph looked back at the women and children weighing down their vehicles.

"Then we'll outrun them," he said. "In the meantime, we'll push ahead as quickly as we can."

Hearing whispers behind him, Joseph turned his head to see two of the Niter Bureau slaves conferring as they walked alongside one of the wagons. Seeing Joseph's gaze, they quickly stopped talking.

Joseph turned back to John and kept walking.

Are those boys up to something? he wondered.

———◆———

Loud banging in the kitchen aroused Charles Davis from a fitful sleep. He quickly sat up on the couch and put his feet on the hardwood floor, momentarily forgetting where he was. It took only a few seconds for him to remember; he stood up and dashed out of the LeConte house to check on the Yankee advance.

Emma, also awakened by the commotion in the kitchen, walked up from the basement in time to see the door slam behind Davis as he fled. *So he did sleep here*, she thought. She went out on the porch and saw him turning the corner at the main campus gate and heading west. Her gaze then moved beyond Davis to the Congaree River, where, on the other side, she could see a group of cavalrymen passing to the front of the pack of Yankee soldiers.

"The fiends," she muttered, stomping back inside. Looking down at the couch so recently evacuated by Davis, she recalled with a little embarrassment her relentless questioning of him from the night before. She'd interrogated him until nearly 3:00 a.m.

Union supplies being brought into Atlanta by caravans that later moved on Columbia

"Mr. Davis," she'd implored, "you must tell me, how will Columbia be treated? Please tell me what you know."

"Miss LeConte, I'm truly sorry but I cannot—I will not—tell you. I can't be the author of your nightmares. It would be too cruel."

She'd not been happy with this answer.

"Seems to me," she said, "that *not* telling what one knows will happen is even crueler."

"Please don't press me on this, Miss LeConte," he'd said. "It doesn't matter what is in store for Columbia—your house and your uncle John and aunt Josie's will be safe."

Jerked out of her reverie by Mary Ann's noisemaking in the kitchen, Emma stepped to the dining room and sat down, joining Bessie and Sallie at the already-set table.

"Sorry, Miss Emma, Miss Bessie, Miss Sallie . . . we gotta be careful with what we got, so it's just gon' be bread and butter this mornin'," she said, bringing in a tray holding toasted bread and freshly churned butter.

The women, looking weary and sleepless, began to pass around the warm bread and spread the butter over it. "Thank the Lord we've still got that cow," Bessie said.

"That poor, sad, skinny cow," Emma sighed, setting off a small rustle of nervous chuckles around the table.

Suddenly the sound of cannon fire erupted in the sky overhead. Sallie leaped out of her chair and backed herself against the wall, trembling, while Emma, Bessie, and Mary Ann ran to the front door.

Outside, a few blocks away from the LeConte house, a shell exploded in the sky.

At the sound of the first shells coming in, Reverend Porter stepped out onto the veranda of Dr. Reynolds's house. Across the river he could see a portion of Sherman's army gathering on the hills outside the city like bees around a hive.

"Anthony!" Magdalen shouted after him from inside. "Where on earth are you going?"

"Won't be a minute," the reverend answered, and just as he stepped down off the porch, he saw a shell strike the corner of the house next door. Screams erupted from the porch of the house, which was crowded with terrified women. Reverend Porter looked down toward Richardson Street and saw throngs of frantic women and children, probably refugees from Charleston like his family and him, walking around and searching for . . . he knew not what.

The sight of so many desperate people out in the streets—unprotected and in the line of fire—appalled the reverend. He determined to go down the street and bring some of them back, to shelter them at the doctor's house. Magdalen would surely scold, but her scoldings usually lasted only a few minutes before her heart took over. As he started to walk, he shielded his head with his hands—he knew it to be a downright ridiculous defense against artillery, but he couldn't stop himself.

The shelling stopped as abruptly as it had started. He paused in the road and gazed out at Sherman's men across the river. Were they moving?

"Sir! Sir!"

Reverend Porter looked around and saw a Confederate officer on a horse looking at him.

"I'm Wheeler," the officer said, and Reverend Porter realized he was talking to Major General Joseph Wheeler of Texas, commander of the Confederate cavalry in South Carolina.

"Anthony Toomer Porter, sir," the reverend replied.

"Can you tell me where I might procure a pair of stockings?" Wheeler asked.

"Stockings?" At first Reverend Porter was confused—why would this major general want stockings? Then he noticed the state of Wheeler's uniform. The pants' legs were ripped and soaked with blood and mud. "Ah! Just so happens I do," he said. "Won't be a minute."

Anthony set off for the store of the Ladies' Relief Association, a charity that distributed supplies—from clothes and books to painkillers, linen, and even liquor—to the sick and wounded soldiers. He talked to the proprietor, Mr. Kerrison, who gave him a box of stockings under the condition that the reverend help get rid of some of the liquor in the store.

"Our boys have already started the looting on their way out of town," Mr. Kerrison said. "And there's no telling what the Yankees'll get up to if they get their hands on this stuff." He pointed to the stacked boxes of port wine in the corner, stamped with the Ladies' Relief Association label.

"Yes, that could be serious," the reverend said. "And those could certainly be of use to the sick over at the hospital. Just allow me to deliver these stockings back to the general, and I'll be back to pick these up. Won't be a minute."

A band of Confederate cavalrymen swarmed the center of town, galloping down Richardson Street. They quickly tied up their horses and, with only a few whispered words between them, began to break into the stores along the street. Any qualms the soldiers might have had about stealing from their own people were swiftly forgotten.

"We risked our lives for this damn war," they said to each other as they began their plunder.

"We ain't had our wages in six months—gotta get paid somehow."

They took to the task as if trained for the purpose, jimmying open the doors, entering the buildings, and, a few minutes later, emerging with cigars, fine cloth, wine, paper goods, foodstuffs, and liquor, which they deposited into their saddlebags.

Shots rang out. A detachment of men emerged from the State House grounds, firing warning shots to disperse the looting soldiers, then moving up Richardson in hopes of disbanding the hordes of looters farther along the street. General Wade Hampton galloped in on horseback and shouted at the unruly men.

"Stop this riotous conduct! That is an order!" Hampton bellowed for backup from his regiment. The looting continued, the men single-minded in their mission. Hampton rode his horse among them, repeating his order. A bleary-eyed cavalryman approached, lifted his weapon, and pointed it at the general's face.

"Just you let it be," he said in a gravelly voice. "Just let it be."

He stepped closer to Hampton as the shelling from the Yankees began again, keeping his weapon in position as his cohort wrapped up their work. Hampton saw whiskey stains on the soldier's uniform and could smell the alcohol on his breath. He looked up the street and could see more soldiers looting farther up Richardson, swarming like locusts.

The cavalryman stepped back from the general, keeping his gun trained on Hampton's head. Looking around he saw some of Hampton's cavalrymen making a noisy approach from a few blocks away. He dropped his arm to his side, holstered his weapon, and took off running back to his horse. Having fortified themselves with as much as they could carry, the Confederate cavalrymen galloped up the street on their way out of town. In their wake a burning cigarette fell onto a bale of cotton on the side of the street, and a thin thread of smoke began to rise.

As he watched the stragglers go, Hampton saw the smoke curl into the air and jumped down from his horse to stomp it out. He looked at the storefronts with their mangled doors and inventory strewn on the sidewalks. Homeless refugees from the low country, to the east of Columbia toward the shore, who'd been milling around the streets, began poking through the wares and creeping into the stores, their entrances made easier by the retreating cavalry.

Unidentified soldier in the Confederate cavalry, outfitted with a rifle, two knives, and two revolvers

"Disgraceful," Hampton whispered. So this is what the war had done to his fellow Confederates—reduced them to drunken marauders, pulling their weapons on superior officers.

As the shelling of the city continued, he looked with worry at the cotton stacked in the street. Two days ago he had ordered the post commander, Captain Green, to move all Confederate and privately owned cotton outside the city to be burned. It was a standing order, after all, that all cotton stores must be incinerated in advance of a Union army incursion. But transporting all the stores proved to be an impossible task, and now Captain Green had fled, leaving the cotton piled in the streets—bale upon bale, stacked high, as far as the eye could see.

One stray spark, one more cigarette carelessly tossed in the street . . . Hampton shuddered.

———————

Henry poked his head out of the front door of the LeConte house. The shelling had stopped and they hadn't heard any explosions for a good hour at least. He had told Emma that it would probably be best if she, her mother, and her sister got their things from upstairs and moved down to the basement so they would be safer when the fighting started again. In the meantime he was going to finish chopping up one of the trees in the yard so that they would have fuel for a fire down there. Looking around, he saw smoke plumes in the air and the battery of Yankee troops across the river. It didn't look like they'd moved, but their numbers were increasing. He cautiously stepped out onto the porch, picked up the ax, and trod lightly to the closest tree.

Inside, Baby Carrie's wails bounced off the basement walls as she writhed in her crib. Upstairs the women collected what little bedding and blankets they'd not sent off with Joseph. Emma walked back into her room to get the pockets she'd made. She slipped into them the few letters she hadn't destroyed as well as some Confederate money. She smiled grimly at the money as she put it away. How much longer would there be a Confederacy in which to spend it?

From her bedside table drawer, she pulled out a locket her father had given her. As she opened it to have a quick look at the daguerreotypes of her mother and father inside, a shell whistled right over the roof and exploded. She stood breathless, instinctively covering her head, waiting for the shell fragments to fall through the ceiling and into her room. She heard Sallie's screaming across the hall, but she was frozen.

"Emma! Emma!"

Emma finally forced herself to move, and she dashed into the hallway. There was Sallie, walking from her room, as pale as a ghost and trembling.

"Oh, Emma, this is dreadful! What are we going to do?"

"Where's Mother?"

"I'm here!" Bessie's disembodied voice sounded from downstairs. "Let's get to the basement!" At that instant another shell sailed close overhead and detonated with as much power as the last. Emma and Sallie barreled down the stairs and followed their mother to the basement.

"Come along, Mary Ann!" Emma yelled into the kitchen as she went down. Mary Ann ran out to the front door to check on Henry outside. She opened the door and there he was, his arms overburdened with the logs he chopped from the tree in the yard.

They rushed downstairs and stood against the wall as the shelling continued, their bodies relaxing slightly when the shelling moved off, then tensing again when it seemed to come nearer. Sallie slumped onto the floor, rocking, her body shaking with fear, while Bessie paced the room with a wailing Carrie in her arms.

When the shelling seemed to have stopped for good, Emma walked to the door, eager to see what was going on outside. But she was stopped in her tracks by a shrieking behind her.

It was Sallie, spitting out jumbles of words, only a few of which Emma could understand: "*Devils . . . fire . . . sky . . . house.*" Sallie didn't seem in control of her own voice.

"I'm here, Sallie! I'm right here!" Emma tried to put an arm around her sister, but Sallie's voice only got louder and louder. "Mother," Emma said, "Sallie's hysterical!"

Bessie bent down to Sallie and placed the crying baby into her arms. Sallie instinctively began cradling the baby and planting kisses on her head.

"Best to give her something to do."

———

"It's stuck, sir. Won't budge."

Joseph looked at Charles, the leader of the Niter Bureau slaves, then down at the wagon wheel that was submerged so deeply in the mud that it was causing the wagon itself to tilt and seesaw. Crossing the swamp was proving harder than he had expected.

"Well," Joseph said, staring back at the other vehicles, "we'll have to unload the wagon and pull it across. It's the only way."

Charles nodded, frowning. "Yes, sir, looks to be the case."

"So, let's get started. John! Johnnie! Captain Green! We're unloading. Charles, tell the others."

The slaves and their families proceeded to empty all the vehicles of their contents. The male slaves paired up and began pulling the wagons across the thick mud, their legs sinking into the sludge as they moved across the soft, swampy ground.

"It'll be getting dark soon," John said to Joseph as they carried boxes behind the wagons. "We should make camp before too long."

"Already?" Johnnie said. "We can't have traveled more than ten miles from Columbia!"

"The boy's right, certainly," Captain Green agreed. "Perhaps it's best, though, to get through this mud and settle in somewhere. Then get an early start for Allston tomorrow."

Joseph sighed. It had been a long day of trudging slowly along roads deep in mud and overgrown with gnarled tree roots. They had taken the Winnsboro Road to Killian's Mill and then, on the advice of some Georgian refugees they encountered, turned onto a crossroad to Allston. This road was in even worse condition, however, increasingly overrun with trees, roots, and bramble bushes. They had struggled on, stalling on endless steep hillsides. Now they were stuck in an unforgiving swamp that forced them to dismantle their tightly packed wagons, pull all the vehicles across the soggy patch of mud, then put it all back together before finding a place to make camp.

But he had to admit, the landscape ahead was the lushest they had seen all day; once they got across this boggy stretch of land, they would enter a deep forest with expansive oak and pine trees, which meant oak leaves and pine straw for bedding, and, with any luck, a stream of pure water.

And, no doubt, plenty of places for Yanks to hide, Joseph thought gloomily.

The tired caravan passed through the sludge as the roar of artillery sounded in the distance.

Reverend Porter slumped on the couch in Dr. Reynolds's living room. Magdalen sat next to him, and Theodore sat cross-legged on the floor with little Anna in his lap. Dr. Reynolds smoked a pipe in his sitting chair, and his wife, Betty, brought cookies in from the kitchen. Everyone listened with uneasy curiosity as the reverend filled them in on what he'd seen.

"That cotton in the street is bad news, surely, don't you think, Dr. Reynolds?" Reverend Porter asked. He'd spent the entire day traveling around, talking to Columbians. After bringing a few boxes of port wine from the Ladies' Relief Association to the house next door, where the women were so frightened that morning, he toted the rest to Dr. Reynolds's house. He would take the wine by wagon to the hospital buildings on the college campus tomorrow morning. All during the day, above and below the city, constant firing kept up between the two armies, and Reverend Porter was relieved to finally be behind closed doors.

A plume of smoke escaped Dr. Reynolds's mouth as he nodded.

"Yes," he said. "But folks want it off of their property. I don't blame them. With this constant shelling, things can catch fire too easily. Better in the street where a fire can be seen and squelched than in a house or a yard where it can spread quickly, before it can be gotten under control."

"Mmm," Reverend Porter responded. "Well, it's lining the street now. I suppose there's nothing to be done but pray."

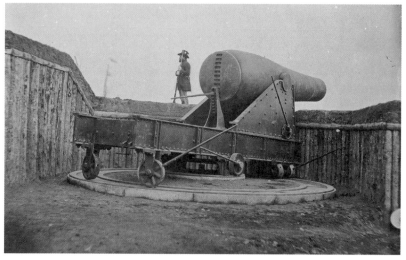

A 200-lb. gun used to shell Charleston; similar guns were turned on Columbia. Photo by Mathew Brady.

"Papa," Theodore said, "we gonna have to leave Columbia, too? Like we left Charleston?"

Reverend Porter and Magdalen exchanged a look.

"Wherever God calls us, we'll go, son," he said brightly. "There are a million places we can go."

"Indeed there are," Betty said, standing up. "The Lord is faithful and has a special plan for all of us." She then walked over to the boxes that the reverend had stacked in the corner that afternoon.

"Now," she said, "who's interested in a splash of wine?"

───────

Sallie had finally gotten Baby Carrie calmed down when a knock came on the door upstairs. Carrie flinched in Sallie's arms, but her eyes didn't even open.

Mary Ann rose from her chair and turned toward the stairs, but Emma stopped her. "I'll go up," she said. She thought she knew who it was.

Sure enough, when she opened the door, there stood Mr. Davis. He was holding something in his hands, but Emma couldn't make it out in the fading daylight.

"A gift for you, Miss LeConte," he said. Emma received it with a look of mild suspicion. It was a collection of multicolored feathers fashioned into a hairclip.

"A gift . . . well . . . thank you, Mr. Davis. Have you . . ."

He slipped past her through the doorway as she studied the curious present.

"Much confusion uptown," he said. "Our soldiers have opened and plundered many stores on Richardson. It's chaotic."

Emma nodded. "We've heard lots of commotion. At least the firing seems to have stopped."

"For the time being." Davis pulled two small figurines out of his coat pocket. "For your mother and sister," he said. "Found all of this in the street."

Emma glanced at the figurines with disdain. What sort of gentleman made "gifts" of items he found on the ground, dropped by a panicked Columbia resident fleeing for her life, or, worse, had stolen outright? She returned her steely gaze to Davis.

Realizing Emma had no intention of accepting the figurines, Davis shrugged and placed them on the hall table. He'd hoped the gifts might lift her spirits, but he saw it would take more than tiny sculptures to put a smile on Emma LeConte's face.

"The bridge will be burned tonight. And the town evacuated of forces."

"And the reinforcements that were coming from Charleston?"

"We cannot hold the town, I'm afraid."

So that's it, Emma thought. *The end is coming*. She wondered what the next few hours would bring and why she didn't feel more terrified. Sallie and Bessie were certainly spooked enough for the whole household. Maybe she was now too exhausted to waste energy being scared. Over the past few months, her emotions had been all over the map. And though her hatred of the Yankees still seethed inside of her, she now just felt . . . resigned.

Through the open door came the shouts of one regiment of Confederates drawn up along the streets on the edge of the campus, ready to march out, the setting sun heralding their departure.

"Our boys are on their way out tonight and tomorrow morning," Davis said. "But I'll be staying behind. I'm arranging for your houses to be protected."

"By whom, if I may ask?"

But Davis refused to answer. "I must be off. I'll check in with you in the morning, Miss LeConte. Please give my best to your mother and sister." He pointed at the figurines on the table. "Don't forget these."

Emma watched Davis jog toward the gates of the campus and turn the corner onto Sumter Street. She walked downstairs to the basement, which was cloaked in darkness except for one candle held by Henry, who was on his way up.

"Miss Emma, I'll stay up and keep a watch on things upstairs. You go on to sleep."

She didn't reply but went directly to the back door that led from the sleeping room out to the backyard. The atmosphere was stifling, with clouds of gunpowder smoke drifting across the lawn, and she thought she smelled something burning. She went back inside and sat beside a gas lantern, opening her diary to start writing. She didn't write for longer than a few minutes before the gas went out and the only light left was the flickering firelight. She fell asleep in the chair, the distant cannon fire crackling in her ears.

She was sleeping soundly at 6:00 a.m. when an explosion ripped through the railroad depot at the southwestern edge of town. The blast shook the ground like an earthquake. Bloodied, charred bodies lay strewn across the grounds of the depot. The single outstretched hand of a burning corpse gripped what had been a loaf of bread and what was now a flaming pile of ash.

3

TRAILS

THE IMPACT OF THE EXPLOSION at the railroad could be felt miles away in Joseph's camp. The ground shook, and Joseph awoke and leaped to his feet in the dim early morning light. A few steps from him, Captain Green leaned against a tree, smoking a cigar.

"I think it's safe to say the invasion has begun," he said darkly.

"What can it mean?" Joseph couldn't believe even the Yankees would launch an assault on an unprotected city. "Our boys aren't even defending the city!"

"It's hard war," Green said, puffing on his cigar. "Sherman's design—bring the war to the home front. Destroy the cities and cripple the will of the people."

I fear to tell you what scenes will be enacted in Columbia. Mr. Davis's words came back to Joseph, now sounding more sinister than ever.

Joseph shivered and turned over, trying to find a comfortable position in his makeshift bed on a pile of straw. As he drifted back into an uneasy slumber, he whispered a prayer for his family.

The LeConte house shook from the explosion. The family was jolted awake by the sounds of shattering windowpanes and picture frames smashing to the floor. Baby Carrie howled, and Emma jumped to her feet and saw Henry peering out the back door to see what he could see.

"Cannon fire?" she asked him.

"No, ma'am, I don't think so."

"I suppose even cannons couldn't make such a noise as that."

"No, ma'am, I reckon not."

Emma looked over at Sallie, wrapped in blankets on the floor, her eyes wide with fright. Mary Ann picked Carrie up and rocked her in her arms, carrying her to their mother.

"It's as sure a sign as we're likely to get," Bessie said, taking Carrie in her arms.

"Sign of what, Mother?"

"Sherman's army intends to put the fear of God in us."

Emma's face darkened as she remembered Sallie's flight from her family's plantation in Liberty, Georgia. Sallie had never confided in Emma about what she'd witnessed, and she bristled whenever Emma questioned her about the trip. But if Sallie's letters from Liberty were any indication, what she saw was grim.

"Oh, Mother, I never want to see them again!" Sallie had written to her family just a few weeks ago. "You must run—run, Mother—if there is even the slightest danger from Yankees."

Father had traveled through hell and high water to rescue her from the Yankees, and he'd only just returned one week ago. Now he was off again, on another treacherous trip behind enemy lines.

Emma gazed at Sallie's face as her sister tried to fall back to sleep. She had no doubt that the Yankees would try to bring Columbia to its knees. And yet she still felt no great fear, only white-hot hatred.

Let them come, Emma thought, almost relishing the idea of what she would say to the enemy soldiers should they try to overrun her house. *I want to see the whites of their devil eyes when I tell them what animals they are.*

She moved upstairs and gazed out the front window, toward the hospital grounds. The sight of shell-shocked, wounded soldiers limping, carrying, dragging one another across the grass had become as familiar as the sight of fresh-faced students in years past. Now there was yet another sad soul hobbling unstably away from an ambulance wagon, wrapped in bloody bandages, his left arm hanging off his shoulder as if barely attached to his body.

"Oh, Father," she sighed, a splinter of fear poking through her veil of hatred. "The horrors of this war are coming home to us now. . . ."

In the early morning light, Reverend Porter picked his way carefully through throngs of panic-stricken people crowding the smoke-filled streets. He'd just finished talking to a cavalryman when he heard a voice calling out to him from the crowd.

"Reverend! Reverend!"

Reverend Porter turned to see an elderly woman calling him over. He approached her with as comforting a smile as he could manage.

Reverend Anthony Toomer Porter, circa 1895

"Do you know what has happened? That terrible noise . . ."

"Yes, ma'am. Not to worry, it wasn't an attack."

She looked at him quizzically.

"An explosion at the South Carolina railroad depot, I'm afraid. There's quite a lot of goods stored there, as well as powder and fixed ammunition, and . . . well, it appears that some folks went there early this morning with lighted torches, to help themselves to goods before the Yankees got here. Somehow the powder was ignited."

The woman gasped.

"The depot was crowded with these desperate creatures, apparently. Many lives were lost."

"Dreadful. Just dreadful," the woman said, retreating back into the crowd.

It was dreadful, the reverend thought. He gazed upon the horizon and saw the coming day lighting up the eastern sky. Looking around through the crowd, he saw a group of Confederate cavalrymen on their horses out in front of Hunt's Hotel. Approaching them, he was surprised to find that Confederate General Wade Hampton was among the men.

"Sir," he said, gingerly stepping up to Hampton, "do you propose to burn this cotton?"

"No, Reverend," Hampton replied. "General Sherman will surely not stay here. He's marked his course with desolation, and he's destroying all the railroads. He'll be pushing on to General Lee's rear in Richmond."

"But surely leaving this much cotton in the streets is asking for trouble," the reverend said.

"It's a hazard, yes. But we gave the order this morning, Reverend: no burning of cotton. I've discussed this with General Beauregard. Now, if Sherman burns the cotton, we cannot help it. He certainly can't take such an amount with him. If he leaves it, it'll be something for our poor people to live on after the war."

After the war. The phrase sounded so strange. Of course, he knew that the war would have to end. How he *dreamed* of it ending. He'd seen with his own eyes the terrors of this bloody struggle during his chaplaincy in the Washington Light Infantry. He himself had survived a plague of measles that had ripped through a Confederate camp where he was serving as army chaplain. Though never an ardent secessionist, he had nevertheless become swept up in the fever that animated his fellow South Carolinians four years ago to withdraw from the Union. He'd even found himself joining in to give the "rebel yell," as it was called, at a secession ratification meeting in Charleston. But when Hampton said these words— *after the war*—it sounded unreal. What would life be like in this new world, without this war that had trailed so much blood and sorrow in its wake? What did the word "peace" even mean now, in a country so divided by hatred, death, and misery?

To the victor go the spoils, he thought, recalling the old saying. *What on earth will go to the defeated?*

Hampton's men lined up for their exodus out of the city. Pausing for a moment, he circled his horse back to Reverend Porter and leaned down to address him.

"I urge you, Reverend, to get notes from the ladies in the city, asking for protection. They'll need it, and I'm sure it'll be given."

"I surely will," Reverend Porter replied. They then bade each other farewell, and the reverend watched Hampton and his men ride out of the city. Columbia's last line of defense was gone.

Just a little way down Richardson Street, Henry and Mary Ann ran to join the other LeConte slaves, who were venturing out to see what could be gotten in the pillage following the last Confederates' departure. All the shops had been broken into, their windows smashed, their doors ripped off their hinges, and their provisions scattered in all directions. Cornmeal, flour, and sugar covered the ground.

"Lord, Henry, look at all that cotton," Mary Ann said, pointing out the bales upon bales of cotton lining the street.

"Huh," Henry huffed by way of reply.

"Henry, what you thinking? You ain't said a word since we left, and when you silent, that mean you thinking too much."

"I *am* thinking, as a matter of fact," he said, shaking his head.

"'Bout what, mister?" Mary Ann sidled up to her husband and threaded her arm through his.

"'Bout what happens when them Yankees come rolling in. All hell gonna break loose."

"What *we* gonna do?"

"*We* ain't gonna do nothing." Mary Ann quickly let go of Henry's arm.

"Henry, you ain't thinking 'bout leaving now, are you?"

After a few seconds of silence, Henry spoke. "Naw. We stayin' right here."

"But you know the talk we heard of black folks' houses bein' plundered just as bad as white folks'. How we gonna live if we ain't got nothing?"

"I reckon we best be as helpful as we can when them Yankees show they faces. Maybe they leave us be, move on to the next house."

"Maybe not, though," Mary Ann said. "Ain't nothing stopping them from doing what they please. I ain't goin' nowhere, though, I'm telling you. And you best not be plannin' to, neither."

Henry reached down and picked up a few sacks of flour to bring back to the house.

"Jest you lift that there sugar and let's get this stuff back afore some other soul gets away with it."

———— ·•· ————

Outside the LeConte house the air was still heavy with smoke from the explosion at the depot.

"I would have thought that there would be another blast coming," Emma said, looking out a basement window. "Yet it's quiet as the grave." She turned to Bessie, who sat at the edge of the couch, knitting furiously, her hands a blur of motion.

"Mother? Why don't you lie back and rest?"

"It was our boys!" Bessie's voice shook as she spoke, and her face was completely wet with sweat and tears. "They must have blown up some stores before evacuating. That's what the explosion was. It was our boys' last act, a greeting to the Yankees. It means they're on their way! They'll be here soon!" She threw her knitting down onto the couch and dropped her head into her hands, weeping.

"Mother," Emma scolded, "we must remain calm. No Yankee should get the better of us; you know that as well as anyone. Now come on, we should try to eat something. Bring your knitting."

Bessie and Emma moved up to the kitchen. Emma felt nauseated and faint from the lack of food—they hadn't eaten since yesterday morning. At the kitchen table, Bessie picked up her knitting, trying to unravel the tangles she'd made.

"I do wish Henry and the others would get back here," Emma said. Seeing her mother struggling with her knitting, she sighed loudly, grabbed the mess of yarn from Bessie, and set to untangling it.

"Honestly, Mother, I don't understand why knitting a blessed stocking is such an unsolvable problem for you! And why do you—"

Suddenly cannon fire exploded—over and over, each blast so near that the *booms* shook the house. The women jumped to their feet.

"It's begun! It's begun!" Bessie ran around the house, checking that all the curtains were closed and the windows locked, while Sallie immediately ran back down to the basement.

"They're coming! Oh, Emma, they're coming! We've got to hide! Come! Back down! Downstairs to the basement!"

Emma secured the pockets she'd sewn for herself under her hoopskirt and followed her mother down the stairs as the cannonading continued.

"Mother! Keep your head on straight, now!"

As she raced down to the basement, Emma heard a desperate pounding on the door. She couldn't see what was out there through the closed curtains, and as she padded over to the door, the banging sounded again.

"Who's there?"

"Oh, Miss Emma! Miss Emma, it's me!"

Emma threw open the door and Mary Ann and Henry bounded in with the provisions they had collected along Richardson Street: sugar, flour, meat, and rice.

"Miss Emma," Henry said, letting the big bags in his arms fall to the floor as he tried to catch his breath, "we hear tell that the mayor has gone to surrender the town."

———————————

Joseph's wagon train lumbered on to Allston as the increasingly rapid cannonading of Columbia sounded in the distance. Joseph couldn't stop himself from envisioning the scene back home if one of those cannonballs should strike his house. What if the roof collapsed, pinning his wife and daughters underneath a pile of timber? He tried to shove these thoughts out of his head as the staccato clatter of the gunning slowly morphed into a continuous roar until, suddenly, it stopped. Distant echoes of artillery slowly dissipated until an eerie silence blanketed the countryside.

Joseph looked at Captain Green and said, "That must mean the surrender of the city."

"Perhaps," Green said.

"Maybe just a break in the fighting," John offered.

"We'll stop here!" Joseph called out to the group. He pointed to a house about fifty yards off the main road and started moving toward it.

"What we stopping for, Master Joseph?" one of the slaves asked.

"I'll see what I can find out about the road to Allston. Hopefully someone here can tell me what's farther along."

"There may be Yankees in that house."

"There ain't no Yankees there," Charles, the head of the Niter Bureau slaves, replied too quickly.

Joseph stopped. Though he trusted his own slaves, he wasn't sure about the Niter Bureau group. He didn't know them as well and could imagine them running off with the Yankees at the earliest opportunity. Is that why they insisted on bringing their families? Was Charles *hoping* to find Yankees in this house?

Joseph decided he had to chance it. They needed to make sure they weren't foolishly heading straight into a Yankee encampment.

The wooden building stood fifty yards off the road, behind an overgrowth of trees and thick foliage. There was no sign of life anywhere. When Joseph knocked on the door, he heard something fall and crash to the floor inside the house. He knocked again. This time, a too-perfect silence. He waited a full minute before knocking one last time. The door immediately swung open, revealing a wild-eyed, terrified face.

"Sir, forgive the disturbance . . . ," Joseph began. The man just stared back with fearful eyes—as if he might run out the back door and climb a tree at any moment.

"Please, sir," Joseph insisted. "I'm not here for any dark purpose."

"You ain't one a' the conscript men?"

"Lord, no." Joseph smiled. "I have no power to arrest you. Is that your fear? Are you wanted for desertion?"

"It wasn't desertion," the man insisted defensively. "At least, not exactly. . . ." He told Joseph that he'd left Columbia at midnight last night and lost his company. He decided it would be safest to come home rather than go back to Columbia.

"We all believed Columbia would surrender today for sure," he said.

"Well, something tells me that may have already happened," Joseph said. "I wonder if you might be able to tell me about the road to Allston. Are Yankees to be found on it, or should we . . ."

The remains of the Congaree Bridge after it was burned by retreating Confederates

But the man was no longer listening. Joseph could see the man's gaze locked on some point in the distance, and he turned to see what was so distracting. A large crowd of motley-looking travelers was overtaking the LeConte wagon train on the road. Some rode in carriages and buggies, some in wagons, but most were on foot. Men burdened with sacks and boxes, some with young children on their shoulders, walked beside the vehicles. Women held babies in one arm while pulling along trains of small children with the other, each child clasping the hand of the next.

Joseph left the man at his doorstep and raced back to the wagons.

"Hallo!" Joseph called to John. "What's the commotion?"

"All fugitives from Columbia," John replied. Joseph looked at the refugees as they passed, surprised not to recognize anyone. Then he saw a familiar face.

"Captain Hughes?" Joseph was shocked to see the condition of his old friend. Hughes had been badly burned; dried clumps of singed purple and blue skin curled off of his hands and face, revealing a soft, shiny pink layer of skin underneath.

"Dr. LeConte! What are you doing out here? Is your family with you? Columbia is no doubt in the hands of the enemy now."

"No, no, my family is at our house on campus," Joseph said, trying not to dwell on the fact. "I'm off to Athens with supplies from the bureau, with a target on my back. What happened to you?"

"Oh, we left Columbia a few hours ago. I was defending the Congaree Bridge."

"So it was burned."

"Yes, by our boys, to cover their retreat. I was nearly burned up with it, as you can see."

The word *retreat* stuck in Joseph's head. Columbia—a city given up for dead, emptied of fathers and husbands, heaving with desperate refugees—now stood completely unguarded against a brutal enemy.

———·•·———

At the Presbyterian Theological Seminary, Reverend Porter sat in a pew in the back of the sanctuary, hands clasped together, praying. He was waiting to get written requests for protection from the dozen Columbian ladies who had come to the seminary for help. He would take these to the generals when the troops entered the city. In the meantime he was relieved to have a moment of relative quiet amidst all the madness.

After his prayers were done, he remained sitting with his head bowed, trying to empty his mind of all that had plagued it over the months since his son Toomer's death. But he knew if he let his mind idle for too long, it might seize upon a painful memory, so he concentrated his thoughts on the one scene that, though it brought him overwhelming sadness, also brought comfort.

Just days before he was stricken with yellow fever, Toomer was as healthy as any other ten-year-old, and he had asked his father to help him fly his kite.

"Papa, come help me raise my kite. I can't do it by myself."

Reverend Porter had been writing a sermon based upon the Bible verse John 4:49, in which Jesus is implored by a royal official to help his dying son: "Sir, come down before my child dies." He had had a sense of foreboding that day, as he'd recently visited many families who had children falling ill with yellow fever. He decided to put down his pencil and go outside to join his son, and he was so grateful that he had. The memories of that

October Saturday when he shared those last carefree moments with Toomer—the boy erupting in laughter as he chased after the kite, his shaggy hair that always needed cutting blowing in the wind, the good humor with which he dusted himself off after tripping and falling—were sacred to Reverend Porter now.

That evening at dinner, Toomer had not eaten.

"I don't feel well, Papa. May I be excused to sit by the fire?" The boy slunk away from the table, and as he left, Magdalen noticed a look of distress on her husband's face.

"Oh, my dear, you are too anxious."

"Don't forget, wife, that there is a pestilence raging," Reverend Porter had replied. He then pushed away from the table to sit with Toomer. "We'll have family prayers and then you can go to bed, my son."

The boy fell asleep during prayers. As Reverend Porter scooped him up to carry him to bed, Toomer said, "Papa, I'm so sorry I slept during prayers, but I'm so tired."

"Put your arms around Papa," the reverend whispered, "and give him one good hug."

Toomer did. It was their last. Seventy-two hours later, as the shelling of Charleston by the Union army began, young Toomer died.

A few tears sprang from the reverend's eyes as the sound of whistling and the rattle of drums yanked him back to the present. He opened his eyes slowly, recognizing the song that was floating on the morning air. It was "Yankee Doodle." He hadn't heard that song in over four years. The Yankees were on their way.

"I'd rather hear the angel Gabriel's trumpet," he mumbled to himself. He hastily gathered as many of the notes that had been written as he could and started for the main street to face the invaders.

————•◦•————

Joseph marched ahead of the wagons. In spite of his fears over his family's safety, he found himself enjoying the glorious morning, which was dry, clear, and warm. The wind was gusty, and the sun shone through the clouds. The slave women and children rode in the wagons, with the men strolling beside them. Joseph had felt a burden lift off of him ever since they had gotten the good news from Captain Hughes that they were unlikely to meet any Yankee soldiers on the way to Allston.

"Uncle Joe!" Johnnie called, running up behind him.

"Johnnie boy! How are you feeling?"

By way of answer, Johnnie coughed and wiped the feverish sweat from his brow. "Great! I'm completely better!" He coughed again.

"Indeed." Joseph smiled. "You sound strong as an ox. But we can take it a little easy this morning."

"Why's that?"

"No use in hurrying—no enemy ahead."

Johnnie nodded, looking up at John and Captain Green, who were riding in one of the wagons a short distance ahead of them.

"Stop, mister, stop!" A woman ran from a cabin a hundred yards from the road, waving her hands as she bounded toward Joseph and the wagon train. "Stop!"

She breathlessly approached Joseph and asked, "Where are you going?"

"To Allston," Joseph said.

"Allston! But don't you know the Yankees are crossing the Broad River not a mile from here? My father expects they'll tear through here any minute!"

Joseph felt his heart pound in his chest. "Impossible! I have it on good authority there are no Yankee soldiers between here and Allston."

"Don't you see that smoke yonder? And that there! And yonder! And again yonder!" The woman turned in a perfect circle, pointing out the smoke trails rising up at points all around them.

Joseph was about to argue when the sound of rifle fire fractured the calm air. He looked up again at the smoke trails and realized the woman was right. Somehow they'd let themselves get surrounded.

Joseph ran as fast as he could, waving his arms and calling for Captain Green and John to stop the wagons. There were Yankees on all sides.

A Horrid Sight

ON THE NORTHERN EDGE OF Richardson Street, the bales of cotton collected by the road were breaking apart. Retreating Confederates had slashed the cording in some, and the bagging of others had been ripped open. A high wind, blowing out of the northwest since early morning, scattered the loose cotton over the ground and into the air. Wisps of cotton snagged on the rough edges of buildings and lodged in trees on both sides of the street. Bundles rolled along the road, gathering dried leaves.

As he and his men entered the city, General Sherman remarked to General Howard that Columbia looked like it was hit by a snowstorm.

——◆——

Captain Green and Joseph peered out from behind a thick clump of pine saplings, watching in tense silence as seven Yankee soldiers approached.

When the shooting started, their group quickly moved the wagons off the main road. The slaves took down a fence that was blocking their entry, allowing the wagons to steer into the brush, then reassembled the fence, carefully erasing their wagon tracks. The group drove deep into the woods and hid the wagons in a thick grove of saplings, continuing on foot a hundred yards farther in and making camp in a little hollow with a stream running through it.

Once the camp was settled, Captain Green and Joseph returned to observe the enemy. From their hiding place among the trees near the main road, they watched as the soldiers approached a house about three hundred yards down the road. A brief burst of gunfire near the house was followed by the sound of squealing pigs and squawking chickens. Soon afterward the soldiers fled, and a plume of smoke rose up behind them.

The two hidden Southerners watched helplessly as a dense column of smoke arose from the house, and then from another house about a hundred yards away. Another and still another column of smoke shot into the sky, as one building after another was lit.

Clouds of dark smoke drifted along the road—Joseph felt the urge to cough but didn't dare, lest he and the captain be discovered. Several Yankee regiments marched within twenty yards of them, and for a moment Joseph was sure they were done for. The two men locked eyes, trying to wordlessly decide their next move: *If discovered, do we surrender? Do we fight?*

The captain slowly reached down for his pistol, getting ready to fire, should the Yankees spot them. Joseph stared at him intently and shook his head. *No. They'll kill us all.*

At the last moment the Yankee troops turned left, up a branch road that skirted the wood.

Soon more columns of smoke rose into the sky—more houses on fire. Federal soldiers continued to pass along the main road. Through his thin protection of leaves, Joseph could see the raggedy

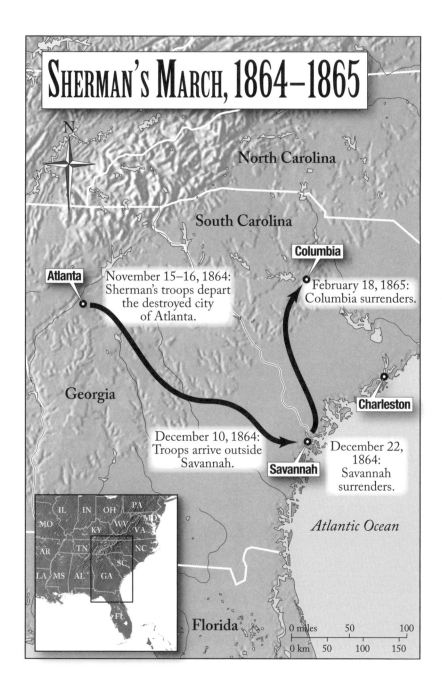

SHERMAN'S MARCH, 1864–1865

N

North Carolina

South Carolina

Columbia

Atlanta

November 15–16, 1864: Sherman's troops depart the destroyed city of Atlanta.

February 18, 1865: Columbia surrenders.

Georgia

Charleston

December 10, 1864: Troops arrive outside Savannah.

December 22, 1864: Savannah surrenders.

Savannah

Atlantic Ocean

IL IN OH PA
MO KY WV MD VA
AR TN NC
LA MS AL GA SC
FL

Florida

0 miles   50   100
0 km   50   100   150

Yankee boots tramping by, the battle-torn uniforms, the scraggly beards of men who've been living outside for far too long. *Them?* he thought. *They are the shabby conquerors sending us scurrying into the bushes?* He and the captain sat frozen, trying to breathe softly.

After the regiment had passed, Joseph whispered, "Wait here." Captain Green looked at him stone-faced and nodded. Joseph crept back to the camp on his hands and knees amid the humming of many voices nearby. He moved carefully, imagining that he was weightless even as he snapped twigs and crunched leaves underfoot, each sound seeming as loud as a rifle shot. When he spotted John and Johnnie, he stood and jogged toward them.

"There are Yankees everywhere," he said softly. "Keep everyone quiet here. No fires." Then he crouched back down and scampered toward one of the columns of smoke on the north side of the clearing. As he got nearer, the smoke got thicker, and he heard the whinnying and stomping of agitated horses. He crouched close to the ground and tried to control the sound of his breathing. Suddenly he heard voices approaching him, and he dove onto his stomach.

Within thirty steps of him passed two more companies of soldiers, leading six horses and mules away from burning stables.

Reverend Porter stood on Richardson Street as the advancing column of the Twenty-Fifth Iowa Infantry Regiment made its way toward him. With so many stragglers falling out of formation, and such a crush of Columbians and refugees out in the streets, he was glad he'd taken the precaution of putting on his clerical clothes. He was able to move freely among the soldiers and the citizens.

The air was full of excitement and confusion. The street was a chaotic mess, with pieces of broken furniture and abandoned merchandise strewn everywhere. As the Federal soldiers fanned out, many people, white and black, rushed out of stores and houses with buckets and pitchers, which the soldiers gladly received. Seeing soldiers passing around these containers and drinking from them greedily, Reverend Porter worried about what exactly was in them.

"What are we giving to these men?" he asked a woman who had just taken a full pitcher to a group of soldiers.

"Drinks to appease the thirsty soldiers, Reverend. We want no trouble from them."

Reverend Porter winced. "These soldiers are thirsty, no doubt. But what are we giving them to drink?"

The woman didn't answer, instead moving off and disappearing into the crowd.

Eager to deliver the letters of protection to the commanding officer, Reverend Porter ran along Richardson until he found Colonel George Stone. Stone was ordering his men to put out a briskly burning fire in a pile of cotton four hundred feet long and three bales high. Two small fire engines had arrived on the scene, and the soldiers worked together with the firemen to control the flames. When Stone finished giving his orders and stepped back from the scene, Reverend Porter seized his chance to approach him.

"Colonel," he shouted in a voice that for the first time betrayed real fear, "the city is filled with unprotected women and children!" He waved the letters that he had been carrying. "I appeal to you as a man of God and a soldier to give me some guards for them."

"Reverend," Stone replied in a steady voice, "you shouldn't worry. Go down to the market house, where my provost marshal is stationed. Please." He gestured toward the letters, and the reverend handed him one. Stone pulled a pen from his coat, and wrote orders on the letter for Reverend Porter to have as many guards as he requested.

Humbled and grateful for the steady calm displayed by the colonel, Reverend Porter thanked Stone and moved on toward the market house on Richardson Street. Stone then set off toward the State House with Captain William Pratt beside him.

On his way Reverend Porter passed a small group of soldiers lounging on a bale of cotton, drinking whisky and lighting their pipes. A spark from one of the pipes fell onto the loose cotton, igniting it. The flames soon spread, and the soldiers hopped up quickly, cursing and stomping on the flames as they fled the fire they'd started.

"Goddammit!" one of the soldiers complained. "You made me spill the whiskey!"

Sitting alone in the back parlor, Emma rocked back and forth in her chair. *Surrender.* Of course she knew that Columbia's surrender had already been confirmed by the fleeing of Hampton's troops. Still, hearing the word spoken out loud—even by Henry—felt like a punch in the gut.

Mary Ann rushed in, throwing open the door.

"Oh, Miss Emma, they've come at last! There's Yankees marching down Richardson Street! And there's a whole slew of women and children around them who seem crazy!"

Furious, Emma ran up to her bedroom and saw through the window the US flag run up over the State House a few blocks away.

"Oh, what a *horrid* sight!" she shouted as the flag thrashed around in the whipping wind. "Lord, I just can't look!" Averting her gaze from the State House, she noticed the high wind blowing hats around the campus grounds. As she stood there watching, a guard arrived on campus to protect the hospital, and sentinels lined up along the wall around the campus.

"So here is our protection," Emma spat as she turned away.

Her emotions turning her face bright red, Emma hurried down the stairs and joined Mary Ann, Bessie, and Sallie, who were all standing at the open door, watching the Yankees coming in.

"First time," Bessie said absently.

"What, Mother?" Emma snapped, irritated.

Bessie came back to herself. "Oh, I just realized . . . this is the first time we've seen Yankees except as prisoners or patients in . . . four years?"

"I can't watch, let's go inside," Emma said. The women were on their way back down into the basement, when a knock came at the door. Bessie paused fearfully, but Emma marched to the door to answer.

"Mr. Davis," Emma said, "thank you for checking on us. Please, come in."

"Miss LeConte," Davis said, stepping inside.

"It's a dark day," Emma said with a sigh.

"I can confirm that the troops in town are a brigade commanded by Colonel Stone. Also, Sherman has promised not to disturb private property. He will lay claim only to the government buildings, but not burn them until tomorrow. Wants to give this wind time to die down."

At this news Sallie clapped her hands, and Bessie heaved a relieved sigh. But Emma's face didn't change. She turned to

Davis, who himself looked dubious about the information he'd just given.

"And you actually believe this?" Emma demanded. "You really trust that Sherman will not punish Columbia for our so-called crimes?"

Backing away, Davis didn't answer. "I just wanted to . . . let you know what I've heard."

Emma rolled her eyes in frustration before composing herself and adjusting her tone. "Well, thank you for your help, Mr. Davis. We are very grateful."

"I've instructed the guards to keep careful watch on your house."

As Davis walked away, the women could hear the yelping of the soldiers surging down Richardson, roughhousing in the street around and inside the State House. Along the northern end of campus, immense wagon trains rolled along Pendleton Street toward the eastern edge of town, where the group would make their encampments.

Emma closed the front door and heard the sound of Carrie crying down in the basement. She looked at her mother, who was white-faced and stricken. "Mama, I'll go."

"Someone must have told Carrie the Yankees have come," she said with a smirk on her way down.

⸺•⸻•⸺

Reverend Porter stood on Richardson Street, in front of the house of the Simmons family, close to the State House. He'd just seen General Sherman walk inside after shaking Simmons's hand and greeting his wife on the porch. The street was full of shouts and laughter, and there was a small fire burning, which a few volunteer firemen were trying to put out.

Reverend Porter wanted to tell Sherman about the chaos he'd seen on the streets, to find out what he would be doing with the cotton, and, most importantly, he wanted to understand what the general's plans were for Columbia. Everyone knew the rumors: Columbia would be reduced to ashes. The reverend couldn't bring himself to believe it. For one thing, he'd met many noble Yankees during his time as an army chaplain. These soldiers weren't the authors of this terrible war; they were just its instruments. He knew in his heart that they weren't all the bloodthirsty animals they were made out to be.

He recalled a time when he was serving as an army chaplain during a terrible measles outbreak in a camp in Virginia. He had ministered to a young Yankee soldier from Rochester, New York,

William Tecumseh Sherman, undated photograph

who was suffering terribly, unable to move from the pain. Reverend Porter had told the young man that he would write to his mother and sisters and tell them that their son and brother was alive and would be cared for.

"Mister, did you say that you came from South Carolina?" the Yankee soldier had asked.

"Yes," the reverend said.

"And you treat a Yankee so?"

"Yes, we are not barbarians. You are a prisoner, but you will be well treated."

"I didn't expect this, and from a South Carolinian, too. If I ever get well, I will fight you no more."

Exchanges like this had convinced Reverend Porter of the essential, oft-forgotten humanity of soldiers forced into battle. Yes, Sherman's campaign was merciless, and his men had committed terrible actions against the Confederates. But as a man of God, Reverend Porter had to hold on to his belief that all men have immeasurable good in their hearts, and this good can come out in the darkest hours. It was this conviction that brought him to this particular house on Richardson Street—he wanted to speak directly to the general himself.

After about twenty minutes, Sherman walked out of the Simmons house, and when Sherman neared the sidewalk, the reverend approached him.

"General Sherman," he said, "I'm army chaplain Anthony Toomer Porter. It's vital that I speak with you."

<hr />

It was early afternoon on February 16, 1865, and twelve thousand Federal troops were in Columbia. Three divisions of the

XV Corps and one division of the XVII Corps were scattered across the city, talking to civilians and seeking out food. Many of them gladly accepted the offer of alcohol.

When Colonel Stone and Captain Pratt returned from the State House, Richardson Street was awash in confusion and disorder. While a dozen of Stone's troops fought the fire in the immense cotton stack, other soldiers ran riot, hooting and hollering, running in and out of stores with looted merchandise. The overall effect was that of a horde of rabid prisoners just released from jail after years in solitary confinement.

"Some of these boys have had too much whiskey," Colonel Stone said.

"Not a surprise," Captain Pratt said. "They haven't slept much in the past two days, haven't eaten in twenty-four hours . . . and now the alcohol."

"They're positively wallpapered," Stone nodded. "This could become debilitating." He surveyed the state of the fire: it looked completely out, except for a few still-smoldering folds. Stone approached the man leading the fire-engine team.

"Sir, I'm Colonel Stone. Who are you? "

"I'm with the Independent Fire Company," the man said. He pointed to a man standing with a hose and dousing a section of smoking cotton. "Palmetto Company. I think we may have this fire beat. With your men's help. Well"—he paused to glare at a group of drunken soldiers falling on top of one another and laughing—"*some* of your men."

"Yes," Stone replied, "it's this damn whiskey they've been given. It's turning them dull-witted and unruly."

"I've just been called away to a fire that's broken out over at the jail. The men here will finish this one up, but I'll need some assistance from your boys. Your *sober* boys."

Stone nodded. "Yes, they'll go with you."

In a few minutes the fireman had set off for the jail with a dozen of Stone's soldiers escorting him. After their departure, Stone turned to Pratt. "We've got to have the alcohol on the street destroyed. Send out the order."

Soon barrels of whiskey were poured into the streets. The alcohol flowed under wagon wheels, settled under cotton bales, and soaked merchandise strewn in the road. Stone and Pratt, with great effort and much shouting, then corralled the inebriated soldiers and force-marched them eastward on Gervais Street to the edge of town where they would make their camp. Still some soldiers fell out of formation, happy to accept whatever whiskey the townspeople would give them. Many did not return to the ranks.

More bewildered Columbians flittered out into the street to watch them leave. No one noticed the tiny flame that had begun to flicker in one of the tufts of whisky-soaked cotton.

———————

Baby Carrie wailed, as she had all day, and the LeConte women took turns trying to soothe her, with no success. Worse, Carrie's coughing fits had returned, and she was struggling to breathe. After her turn with the baby, Emma had gone upstairs to the third-floor balcony, where she gazed out at the woods along the southeastern edge of the city for what seemed like an eternity. It was a more peaceful view than she would be afforded on the north side of the house, where the windows looked out on rowdy

Yankees wreaking havoc on the city—with blacks in the streets egging them on—or horribly wounded soldiers being brought in to the hospital, some without arms or legs, others with head wounds that had rendered them dumb or blind, most howling in mortal pain.

But the view of the woods as she sat on the balcony was a welcome change. The wind blowing through the dense woods always calmed Emma. And even with the shrieking of her baby sister sounding from down below, she was soon lulled into an uneasy half sleep. The daylight began to dim around her as she dozed in her chair. She was falling deeper and deeper as the baby's screaming and coughing got louder and louder. Suddenly a voice jolted Emma awake.

"Emma! Emma!" It was Bessie. She'd come out to the balcony holding Carrie in her arms. "She won't stop coughing, and look at her face!"

Emma looked at her baby sister. Her rash had returned, and blotches of red now covered her cheeks and forehead. "She's getting worse," Emma whispered.

"What are we going to do, Emma? We've got no more Dover's powder!" Emma took Carrie from her mother and lowered her head toward her sister's face: it was boiling hot.

"I'll go out and get Dr. Thomson," she said.

"Miss Emma! Miss Emma!" It was Henry, calling from downstairs.

Emma jerked her head around and saw the horizon lit up with campfires. Beyond the woods she could see General Hampton's stately house a few miles in the distance, wrapped in flames. She turned toward the river and saw another blaze engulfing buildings near the river and illuminating the night sky with an orange glow.

"Oh, dear God!" Emma handed Carrie back to her mother and hurried inside and down the stairs and saw Henry running in the front door.

"Miss Emma, there's a terrible fire on Richardson Street!"

Out on the front porch, Emma saw flames shooting up from beyond the campus walls. Sumter Street was also lit up by a burning house a few blocks away, so near to the LeConte house that she could feel the heat from the blaze. She and Henry watched as soldiers staggered about the streets, screaming and noisily singing songs, their faces glowing with a red glare from the flames around them.

"Emma! Emma? What's happening?" Bessie shouted, shuffling down the stairs with a yowling Carrie in her arms.

"Fire on Richardson, Mother!" Emma yelled, hurrying back into the house with Henry. "The hellhounds are making themselves at home."

Emma could see smoke rising behind the hospital buildings—exactly where she needed to look for Dr. Thomson. How close was the fire to the hospital? Could she get there and back before Carrie stopped breathing altogether?

"I'll try to be quick," Emma said, stepping off the porch.

"Emma, no!" Bessie shrieked. "Send Henry!"

Henry stepped forward, but Emma shook her head.

"No, he should stay to protect the house. Henry," she said, turning to him, "get everyone down to the basement. And don't let them out."

———⋯———

Reverend Porter arrived back at Dr. Reynolds's house to find that several families from the neighborhood were huddled in the sitting room along with Dr. and Mrs. Reynolds, Magdalen, Theodore, and little Anna. A captain of the Federal Army, who was sent to guard the house, met the reverend at the door with a stern look. Everyone looked at the guard as if he were holding them prisoner rather than offering protection.

"That is my family," the reverend said, pointing to his wife and children. The guard let him through and he walked straight into his wife's arms.

"Anthony, you're safe!" Magdalen cried out. "You must stay with us now. No more running around!"

"I'm sorry, dear, but I had to do what I could to help," he said. He then turned and addressed the room. "I've spoken with General Sherman." This news captured everyone's attention.

"So, you spoke to the devil himself," one of the neighborhood women scoffed.

Reverend Porter ignored the comment. "He seemed to deeply deplore the situation in town." At this the woman rolled her eyes. "He said that it is his duty as a soldier," the reverend continued, "to stamp out the rebellion, as he terms it, whomever it hurts. But he wanted me to tell the ladies of Columbia that they are as safe as if he and his men were a hundred miles away."

"Oh, is that so!" the woman snapped angrily, standing up and stomping her foot. "Go on the roof of the house and see for yourself."

Reverend Porter and the Union captain obeyed, ascending the stairs and exiting through the skylight window to the Reynolds's roof, where they saw a circle of flame around the city. The reverend gasped.

"No, those are only campfires," the captain insisted.

"No, sir!" the reverend said, his voice tightening. "I've seen many campfires in my time as an army chaplain, and I know what one looks like. Those are houses, Captain! I know those houses. That one belongs to George Trenholm, that one to General Hampton, that one to Colonel Wallace. They've been deliberately set aflame!"

At that moment they saw another fire break out on Richardson Street, near Washington. As the flames spread, three small hand engines arrived on the scene. Suddenly plumes of flame shot into the sky. As Reverend Porter watched in horror, eight more fires broke out simultaneously across the northern streets of the city.

The reverend gazed out at the street, then grimly pointed down. A small group of soldiers swarmed around the fire engines, smashing them and cutting their hoses.

"What would you call that?" he asked the captain. The man took a long look, then scurried over to the skylight.

"Where are you going?" Reverend Porter demanded as the captain quickly disappeared back into the house. "Come back! We need protection!"

A gale of wind sent the reverend sprawling to his knees, and when he picked himself up, he saw that the city was wrapped in a sheet of bloodred flames.

His heart beating wildly, he hurried down the steps to the sitting room.

"Our fears are realized," he said, his voice trembling. "Columbia is on fire."

THE GATES OF HELL OPENED

EMMA FRANTICALLY BOUNDED THROUGH THE dimly lit main hall of the campus hospital, searching for Dr. Thomson. Men with bloody and bandaged bodies lay in cots, while those who still had use of their legs stood at the windows, watching the flames lighting up Richardson Street.

Emma approached a soldier standing at the window with his back to her. "Excuse me . . . I'm looking for Dr. Thomson. Do you know where he is?"

The soldier turned toward Emma and she gasped. There was a coin-sized bullet hole in his cheek. His right cheekbone and right lower jaw were broken, causing the whole side of his face to collapse and droop as though he were not a man but a melting wax figure. He pointed at a nurse who was passing by with a tray full of bloody towels, then turned back to the window without saying a word.

Emma rushed up to the nurse. "Excuse me, please. I need to find Dr. Thomson. My baby sister has measles and her cough is terrible and she's—"

"He's not here," she snapped. "Went outside to help with the fires."

"I need Dover's powder," Emma pleaded. "Is there any here? He had some in his case the last time he came to our house."

"We can't give up anything we have—we've got more patients than we can handle."

"Please, miss, please!" Emma begged. "I don't know what else to do!"

The nurse scuttled away out of the main hall. Cursing under her breath, Emma scampered up the stairs. She sped down the narrow hallway on the second floor, whipping her head left and right, looking for doors that might lead to supply closets. Midway down the hall she came to a door that had been left ajar. She stepped into a small room that had a sink, a counter, and a large window through which Emma could see flickers of orange. She rushed to the window and got a view of the scene on the street.

Although night had fallen, the sky over Columbia shone with a sinister glow. Soldiers swarmed the roads, staggering through downtown stores and houses, hunting for food, drink, and loot. Multiple fires were burning up and down Richardson Street, and a single fire company was overwhelmed with trying to put them out. Flames engulfed bales of cotton that had been piled high just west of the State House, and the now-furious wind sent tufts of burning cotton flying into trees, through windows, and onto wagons.

Sparks flew, and bales ignited before her eyes. She saw men run into a store and back out minutes later, escaping the flames that soon overtook the building. On upper Richardson, violent red flames shot out of every window of the Congaree Hotel with a furious roar. Next door one of the Confederate government office buildings surrendered to the inferno's attack, buckling and swaying and, finally, collapsing. Screams of people in the street filled the air as it went down.

One giant, angry conflagration roared in front of her eyes. Emma stepped back from the window and wiped away tears. For a terrifying minute she'd forgotten all about her sister's medicine.

———•◦•———

At their camp deep in the woods, Joseph sat down on the ground where John, Johnnie, and Captain Green were clustered around a lantern, their faces lit with a flickering orange light. He'd just returned from his lookout, where he'd spent the last few hours keeping tabs on the Yankees' movements. The slaves were huddled nearby with a few lanterns lit, and Joseph could hear them whispering to each other. A few of the slave children wept as their mothers tried to quiet them.

"It's been a few hours since I last saw a Yankee out there," Joseph told the other men. "I think they may have moved on."

"If they've gone we can leave early in the morning," Captain Green said.

"Master Joseph," a male voice said out of the darkness. It was Sandy, one of his slaves.

"Yes, is that you, Sandy?"

"Yes, sir. I wanted to ask, sir . . . the children are awful hungry. We need to fix them some food."

"Give them some hardtack."

"Ain't no hardtack left, Master Joseph."

Joseph sighed. "So you're saying you want to light a fire."

"Not *want* to, sir. *Need* to."

"John, what do you think? Maybe if they keep it small?"

A rolling of drums wafted in on the wind, followed by the sound of cheering. A party of Union soldiers was returning. They had not moved their camp after all. John looked sternly at Joseph and shook his head.

"I'm afraid we can't let you do that, Sandy," Joseph said.

"Why, sir?"

"Dammit, you can hear why, Sandy," John blurted out. "The Yankees are coming back. We can't afford to risk them seeing your campfire."

"But sir, the children ain't had no food since this morning."

Sandy waited for a reply, but none came. He stood silently for a moment and then slunk away, back to the slaves' encampment to deliver the bad news.

"What are we to do now, gentlemen?" Joseph sighed. "With these Yanks back it appears we're stuck here until they decide to move. No telling when that will happen."

The other men remained silent as the sounds of the soldiers' merriment got louder. Soon their fires were visible on the Broad River, about a mile away. The drums and cheering heralded party after party returning laden with plunder.

"Has it struck you," Captain Green said, "that we might have been better off bringing our families with us? More mouths to feed, but at least we'd know . . ."

"That they were safe," Joseph finished. "Yes, Captain, I've thought of that. God knows what's happening in Columbia right now. Emma is steady and strong, but Bessie and Sallie . . . well, they're more fragile."

"Master John." A woman emerged from the darkness with two other women following behind. It was one of the Niter

Bureau wives, and she strode up to the men with a determined air. "We must cook food for our children. They hungry."

John looked at Joseph, who threw up his hands.

"We said no." John scowled. "The Yankees will see the fire, and we'll be discovered."

"If we don't get any food in our children's stomachs, the Yankees will be hearing their cries, Master John. The *children's* cries. And it gonna get *loud*."

Joseph and John exchanged worried looks.

"Fine," Joseph said. "A *small* fire. And well hidden. Tell the boys to make sure of it."

The slaves then set to work making a fire and constructing a thick screen of boughs that would help conceal it. Within twenty minutes it was burning briskly. The women set to frying up fatback and johnnycakes, and as the scent of the frying cornmeal reached Joseph's nose, he worried about the Yankees catching a whiff as well. *How far can a scent travel?* he wondered. Then he looked up and saw something even more distressing: the campfire's reflection in the treetops.

Emma rummaged through the cabinets and drawers of the hospital supply room for anything that might ease Carrie's cough. Bandages, droppers, towels . . . nothing useful. Slamming a drawer shut, she stepped back over to the window. The fires looked ready to devour every structure on Richardson.

Anger surged within her. She knew in her heart that these fires were not accidents but a plan passed down from Sherman himself to destroy Columbia. Yes, the wind and the cotton in the streets were doing their part to spread the blazes, but what about the soldiers she'd seen running around wildly, plundering stores and houses that suspiciously caught fire just as they exited?

Emma had looked through every drawer and cabinet in the room and come up empty. As she raced out the door and down the darkened hallway to try to find another supply room, an explosion sounded nearby. Outside the window she saw flames shooting into the air over Phillips Warehouse on the north part of Richardson. A few seconds later came another explosion, this one closer.

She dashed down the stairs, through the makeshift infirmary full of moaning patients in cots, and out to the main door. A screaming patient, running in the opposite direction, slammed into her, sending her sprawling on the floor.

"It's all on fire! We'll all burn!" he shrieked. Three nurses grabbed hold of him and pulled him back to his cot as he flailed about and tried to squirm out of their grasp. Emma stood and darted out the door into the lobby. There, leaning against the wall, breathing heavily, was Dr. Thomson.

"Doctor!" she shouted. "I was looking for you—we need medicine for Carrie!"

Dr. Thomson wiped sweat from his brow and, Emma thought, tears from his eyes.

"What is it, Dr. Thomson?"

"I've been helping with the water hoses," he said. "Fires are popping up everywhere."

"Yes, the Yankees are doing the devil's work," Emma said. "It's ghastly."

Dr. Thomson nodded absently.

"Doctor, please, could you come look at Carrie? We're out of Dover's powder. Her cough is frightfully bad, and we . . ."

She couldn't finish the thought. The screams of the panicked patient in the infirmary filled the empty space.

A bell clanged a few blocks away, signaling the arrival of another fire truck.

"Dr. Thomson, there're more firemen. . . . Please, can you come with me to the house?"

Dr. Thomson nodded. "Miss Emma," he said, "this inferno's devouring the city. And there isn't enough water on earth to stop it."

"Please, Dr. Thomson," she pleaded, quickly wiping tears from her eyes. "Please, let's hurry. Carrie can't breathe. . . ."

Dr. Thomson didn't answer. He appeared as if in a trance, his glassy eyes staring straight ahead, his breathing labored and wheezy.

"Dr. Thomson!" Emma blurted out, startling the doctor and shaking him out of his dark reverie. "The fires may be burning, but my baby sister is dying! Please!"

Dr. Thomson inhaled deeply and wiped soot from his face. He stumbled over to the examination table where he'd left his medicine case, picked it up, and turned to Emma.

"Let's go."

———•◆•———

The blaze spread quickly up and down Richardson, Gervais, Washington, Sumter, and Lady Streets and inched toward the Reynolds house. Inside, the families began gathering their things together—it had been decided they would leave to seek cover farther from the blaze.

"Everyone please remain calm." Reverend Porter tried to project a sense of composure over the rumbling of anxious voices.

"This house is brick. I think unless it is itself set on fire, we will probably be safe."

"These demons want us burned to a crisp, all of us!" one of the neighborhood women shouted.

"Darling, remember what they did to Atlanta!" Magdalen said, holding a crying Anna in her arms. "Oh my God, they burned it to the ground! Where has our guard gone?"

Reverend Porter's faced twitched with frustration. He had truly believed that the Yankees would not do to Columbia what they had done to Atlanta. He'd met Sherman—spoken to the man, even. Looked him in the eye. The reverend had been certain that the general was not an evil man. But this chaos and the heat from these fires could not be denied. And it was spreading so fast. He suddenly felt a sense of panic—how close were the flames now?— and bolted outside to make sure they weren't in immediate danger.

"Papa, where are you going?" Theodore shouted.

"Won't be a moment, son, not to worry. Papa's got to check that we're safe."

He scrambled out onto Washington Street and headed west toward Richardson, which was engulfed in flames now. Washington and Sumter Streets brimmed with Yankee soldiers, mounted and on foot; some appeared sober, but many were in every stage of drunkenness. Threading through them was a grim parade of pale-faced women, some with infants in their arms, leading terrified children away from their burning houses on Richardson, their faces stricken with fear. The wind whipped through their hair and clothing, and sparks shot through the air. The women shielded their screaming children from the flaming debris, moving along the street silently, no sound escaping their lips, no tears rolling down their cheeks.

The burning of Columbia, as illustrated in *Harper's Weekly* shortly after the incident

Around them soldiers jumped and shouted. "Look at the aristocrats now!" they barked. "Left by their cowardly husbands to burn!" The women didn't flinch or show the least awareness of the insults being hurled at them.

Men have become beasts, Reverend Porter thought. Had he been wrong about the Yankees?

The wind blew a gale of heat and fire around the reverend, hurling flames from house to house with horrifying speed. The fire spread across roofs, into windows and doors, and against fences. Blazing siding sailed onto the roofs of buildings. Searing shingles shot in every direction. Brick walls fell, barrels of liquor burst, and the wind howled. Two blocks away, the flames reached the storage warehouse of ammunition and shells, setting off multiple explosions that shook the ground and inflamed the surrounding buildings.

"The gates of hell have opened upon us," Reverend Porter whispered.

———————

Back at the LeConte house, Emma watched the expanding inferno from the front parlor window looking out over the porch. Hearing footsteps on the basement stairs, she turned and saw Dr. Thomson step into the room, fastening his medical bag. Downstairs, Carrie continued coughing.

"I've given little Carrie some syrup with Dover's powder," Dr. Thomson said. "Hopefully that will help. Keep her bundled up, and I've left you some more powder downstairs."

"Thank you, doctor." She gestured out the window. "I think the fires have reached the State House."

The LeConte house was separated by only four city blocks from the growing blaze on Richardson. The flames began to lick the edges of State House square, and the strong winds blew flames in every direction—it was impossible to tell which direction the firestorm would turn next.

"I should get back," Dr. Thomson said. He tipped his hat to Emma and disappeared out the door.

Emma watched him scurry back to the hospital. She could see Yankees standing guard all along the periphery of the campus, with about six clustered at the campus gate, but none had intruded on the LeConte family. Just as well, she thought; she didn't know how she would react if she were forced to speak to one of them. "I'd sooner eat my own tongue," she thought.

"Emma!" It was Bessie, calling from the basement. "Emma, darling, Aunt Josie has come!"

Aunt Josie! She lived on the north end of campus, nearer the flames. Was her house safe, or had she fled?

Emma gazed out the window one last time before joining the others, expecting that the fire would already have come closer. But—was she imagining this?—instead of approaching the LeConte house, the fire seemed to be moving away. The lurid red glow and giant, maniacal flickering of flames on the other side of the State House seemed to be dying down. For a moment Emma thought perhaps—maybe—they'd seen the worst of it.

"Looks like the danger is over, Miss Emma," Henry said, walking into the front room. "The fires will be under control soon, I reckon."

"Oh, Henry, is it true?" She didn't quite believe him, though he sounded so confident.

"Yes, ma'am. You see?" He pointed out the window. "No more fires on the other side of the State House. I think it's dying down. You should go down and get some rest."

Though she couldn't quite bring herself to believe that the worst was over, she was so worn out with fatigue and excitement that the thought of even a minute of rest was irresistible. She went downstairs and told everyone of Henry's prediction as she climbed onto the couch, her eyes barely open.

"Wishful thinking," Josie said, shaking her head.

"Josie's house is safe, sweetheart," Bessie said.

"Oh, Auntie, I'm so relieved," Emma said, sighing.

Bessie knelt beside the couch and stroked her daughter's head. Emma quickly sank into a heavy sleep. She dreamed that she was sleeping in her bed and that her father was sitting at her bedside, stroking her head. She opened her eyes just a sliver and could see his face, looking sweetly at her.

"Oh Father," she said, reaching out to him. "You're back. We've been so worried. . . . I think Mr. Davis has the measles." She heard crying. She tried to open her eyes wider to see but she couldn't. Her father had begun to cry in front of her, sitting there by the bed, hunched over. She tried to grab hold of him, but he kept moving out of reach. His crying got louder until it became a wail. He raised his head and blood trickled out of his eyes.

Emma's eyes popped open, and she was once again on the couch in the basement. But the wailing remained.

She turned and saw that it was coming from someone standing by the fire. Squinting, she realized it was Mrs. Caldwell, her neighbor. Bessie and Sallie hovered around her, trying to offer comfort. She was wrapped in a blanket, her body shaking.

Mrs. Caldwell turned around and saw Emma sit up on the couch.

"Oh, Emma! Our home is on fire! The flames are licking at the campus walls!"

"We've got to get out of here!" Betty shouted when Reverend Porter returned to the Reynolds house. "Our guard has deserted us, and the house next door is burning! The blaze is going to take every house!"

"But where are we supposed to go?" Magdalen asked.

"The Duncan house!" Betty responded. "That's where Sherman's headquarters are. Right, Reverend?"

"Yes, this is true, he is staying with the Duncans. I suppose we could—"

"So, we go there and demand protection." Betty tried to corral everyone outside. "Let's go!"

"Go to the house where General Sherman is staying?" Magdalen asked. "How is it possible to make demands like that? Who are we that he'll even listen to us?"

"We must!" Betty said. "His headquarters certainly won't have been burned—his villainous men would have made sure of that. So we go and demand sanctuary."

"But we can't leave our house!" Dr. Reynolds shouted, looking at his wife in a panic.

"Bill," Betty scolded, "don't be a fool. It's only a matter of time until this house is burned!"

Dr. Reynolds was paralyzed. If he left his home, he would be relinquishing it to the flames. But what else could they do?

"Hurry!" Betty said.

Reverend Porter dashed to the guest room and crouched down beside the bed. He took his church's silver service tray, which he'd brought with him from Charleston, out of its box, placed it in an open box under his bed, and threw a towel over it. While he did this, Magdalen gathered some clothing and blankets for the children.

Theodore bent down next to Anna.

"It's piggyback time, Anna! You ready?" Anna's eyes were red from crying. Her face was tilted downward and she didn't answer.

"Anna-girl, are you gonna say no to a piggyback ride?" Theodore said, trying to swallow his own fear. Anna shook her head and wiped tears from her eyes with her curled up fingers.

"Good." Theodore smiled, turning his back to her. "Get in position!"

After a moment of uncertainty, Anna threw her arms over his shoulders, and Theodore, still stooped, lifted her up onto his back.

"Ready, Anna," he said. "Five, four, three, two, one . . ."

"Squeak, piggy, squeak," Anna blubbered.

Theodore sighed. "Come on, Anna, you can do better than that! Five, four, three, two, one . . ."

"Squeak, piggy, squeak!" she squealed. Theodore jumped up and ran out onto the porch. The entire group set out into the blazing streets, heading east on Washington. They trudged through the howling mass of Yankee soldiers and Columbian refugees, dodging flying embers and blazing debris as they made their way through the chaos. The smoke stung their eyes, and the searing bright light from the crimson flames gave the soldiers' faces a devilish glow.

"Where's Bill?" Betty shrieked, realizing Dr. Reynolds was no longer beside her. She whipped around to look for him, her eyes smarting at the brightness of the surrounding flames. "Bill!"

A group of soldiers were clustered on the side of the street, laughing and jostling.

"Which way are you going?" she heard one of them shout. Looking closer, she saw that he was talking to her husband.

"You going that way?" the soldier said, pushing Dr. Reynolds to the left. "Or this way?" He swung him back to the right.

"Get your hands off him, you vile creatures!" Betty said, storming up to the group and seizing the arm of her confused and dizzy husband. "This is how you treat an old man, is it?"

One of the soldiers bowed in an exaggerated fashion. "I'm ever so sorry, your highness."

Betty spat in his face. The man moved to strike her but his fellow soldiers held him back.

"Disgusting pigs," she said and hurried with Dr. Reynolds back to join the others.

"Darling," Dr. Reynolds whispered, dizzy from being shoved around, "we've got to go back . . . back to our house . . . it's all we have."

"Out of the question, Bill," Betty said. "It's likely already burning."

They caught up with the others and at last reached a block of houses on the eastern end of town that was untouched by fire. Squinting through the sudden dimness, Reverend Porter realized that they were near the house of a friend, Raymond Miot, which sat on Lady Street, within a block of General Sherman's quarters.

"Let's try to stop here," the reverend said to the group. "Raymond will certainly allow us refuge." They walked to where the Miot house sat on the corner of Pickens and Lady. Tied to the gate of the house stood two bridled military horses, their owners nowhere in sight.

"Please, come in, come in," Mr. Miot said when he saw Reverend Porter on the porch, the beleaguered refugees behind him. Once they were all safely inside, Dr. Reynolds hurried back over to the door, looking alarmed and distracted.

"Bill," Reverend Porter said, "are you all right? Why don't you sit down."

Dr. Reynolds looked back at the reverend, his eyes glazed with panic. Reverend Porter reached out for his friend, but Reynolds backed away from him, then turned and bolted out of the house.

"Bill!" Betty screamed.

"Betty, I'll go after him," the reverend said, stepping in her path. "Please stay where you're safe." He then dashed out the door and leaped over the porch steps to the front yard in pursuit of his friend. "Bill!" he shouted.

"I have to go back home!" Dr. Reynolds screamed, without slowing down or even turning his head to be heard. "My whole life is there! All we have! I can't leave it!"

"Bill, no! Come back!"

As the reverend's eyes started to sting, he saw a blurry Dr. Reynolds disappearing back into the thick curtain of smoke.

Emma tried to get comfortable on the blankets she'd laid out on the basement floor. She closed her eyes and felt a sickening despair. Sallie sat on the floor against the wall, rocking back and forth, chattering nonsense. Bessie slumped on the couch and stared at the burning embers in the fireplace, while Josie sat beside her, stroking Bessie's hand. Mrs. Caldwell, in a rocking chair in a darkened corner of the room, was still weeping quietly. Carrie, mercifully, had finally fallen asleep. Though they were desperate for news, they were terrified of going outside. No one dared even look out the window, for fear of what nightmares might lurk there.

Footsteps sounded on the staircase, followed by Mary Ann's voice.

"Miss Emma?" Drifting into sleep, Emma didn't answer.

"Miss Bessie!" It was Henry's deep voice this time. Bessie looked up from the fire as if awakened from a dream.

"Miss Josie's house," Henry bellowed from the top of the stairs. "It's caught fire!"

At this news the women all sprang back to life, jumping up and running upstairs. Emma threw open the front door, and they all spilled out onto the porch, where they could see, three blocks to the northwest, a blazing scene. The State House was one grand conflagration, and the searing yellow flames were leaping onto the campus buildings on the north side.

Wordlessly, Josie stepped out onto the porch and down the steps, walking determinedly toward her house in the shadow of the inferno.

———•◆•———

Charles Davis, dressed no longer in Confederate gray but Yankee blue, hurried down Pendleton Street, trying to put distance between himself and the blaze at the State House. He turned his head and nodded at the two soldiers following after him. He waved to them, then pointed up ahead at a house on the college campus at the corner of Pendleton and Sumter—John and Josie LeConte's house.

"That's the one," he said.

The soldiers rushed up the porch steps.

Night Turned to Noon

THE SKY WAS A QUIVERING molten ocean. Searing white flame engulfed the State House. Columns of black, rolling smoke glittering with sparks and flying embers swept across the copper-colored sky. All around the State House, dense showers of burning flakes exploded and sparkled. Solid masses of flames had walled off the center of Columbia, and the otherworldly roar of the blaze clashed with the crunch of crashing timbers and the thunder of falling buildings.

Night had turned to noon.

The hospital buildings all along the north side of campus had caught fire. Physicians and nurses scuttled along the roof with buckets of water, trying to douse the spreading flames. Wounded inmates crawled out of the hospital windows, screaming for help for the patients inside who couldn't move.

At the LeConte house Bessie was hysterical. "The house is doomed! We've got to get away! We can't wait for Josie any longer!" Grasping Baby Carrie and yanking Sallie by the hand, she hurried into the back garden, far from the house. "Emma, please! You must come!"

Emma stood at the front door, mesmerized by the inferno. She turned to see Mary Ann and Henry standing behind her, their eyes fixed on the burning State House. Seeing the family slaves standing there watching Columbia burn, she was consumed with rage.

"Are you two happy now?" she said, stepping toward them. "Is this what you all wanted, to bring these Yankee animals down here, to tear us all apart?"

Shocked by the outburst, Mary Ann and Henry took a step back in unison.

"Burn our homes, kill us, do even worse?"

"No such a thing, Miss Emma," Henry said softly. "No such a thing."

"What did you all think this would accomplish? Do you really think that the Negroes up north are better off than you? Working fourteen-hour days in filthy factories, their children starving, their backs bent, never seeing the sun?"

Henry grabbed Mary Ann's hand and looked down at the floor. He didn't want to cause more pain to this young lady he'd watched grow up, this child who knew everything but understood nothing.

"You answer me, Henry! What makes you think their lives are so much better than yours?"

"Their lives are their own, Miss Emma," he said calmly. "Ain't about better or worse. Their lives are their own."

———

"Bill! Bill!" Reverend Porter ran through the hazy street, trying to catch up with Dr. Reynolds, his eyes burning from the thick smoke. He stopped to catch his breath and could hear Magdalen calling after him from the Miots' house.

He rubbed his wet eyes, and as they began to clear he saw that a man a few feet ahead of him was bent over, wheezing, his hands grabbing his knees.

"Dr. Reynolds, is that you? Bill?"

"I've got to get back to my house, Anthony," Dr. Reynolds said between deep breaths. "It's all I have."

Reverend Porter helped his friend stand up, and they took a few halting steps, right into the path of a stone-faced Yankee officer.

"Nothing but flames that way, gentlemen," he said. "I suggest turning back."

"I've got to get home," Dr. Reynolds panted.

"Sir, where is your home?"

Dr. Reynolds was too winded to answer.

"He lives on Washington Street," the reverend interjected. "Washington and Marion."

The officer, Lieutenant John McQueen, looked in the direction they were headed, then back at Reverend Porter. He shook his head. The reverend realized the lieutenant had no idea where he was.

"It's one block this way," Reverend Porter said, pointing beyond a group of soldiers, who were thick on the smoky street, drinking, roughhousing, and shouting at civilians. More and more were entering town from their camps in the east, drawn to the spectacle of the flames and the promise of alcohol.

"Sir," McQueen said, "I urge you not to venture that way. The wind is blowing wildfires, and these men cannot be trusted to leave you be. Moving among them will only encourage aggression."

"The man is right, Bill," Reverend Porter said. "Let's go back to the Miots', where it's safer."

"No, I've got to get our valuables before either the Yankees or the fire claim them."

"Then I'll escort you," McQueen said, gazing disapprovingly at the soldiers cavorting in the streets. "Company discipline appears to be at low tide. You'll need protection."

"Whatever you like," Dr. Reynolds said, stumbling ahead without waiting. McQueen nodded at the reverend. "Go back to the house. I'll make sure he stays safe." He then quickly set out to catch up to Dr. Reynolds.

Wondering whose hands he had delivered Dr. Reynolds into, Reverend Porter watched them disappear into the murky, lawless street.

———————

Josie LeConte stood outside her house, staring at the open front door. She certainly had not left her own front door ajar. . . . So who was inside?

The house was not burning, though when she placed her hand on the front porch railing on her way up the stairs, it was hot to the touch. She heard footsteps inside and saw a guard blocking the doorway, but nevertheless she scurried in to get out of the heat. She smacked into a Yankee guard who'd stepped into her path.

"This is my home," she said to him. "I'm Josie LeConte." The guard wordlessly stepped aside to let her pass.

"Miss Josie," she heard a voice say. Looking around the living room, she saw Andrew, one of her slaves, standing against the far wall with a bucket in his hands. He'd been dousing the walls with water to keep them from catching fire. "I so glad you safe."

"Andrew, how many men have been here?"

"'Bout five, I reckon." At that moment four Yankee soldiers stumbled onto the porch and bounded through the door.

"The roof is on fire!" one of them bellowed at the guard. "I just saw flames up there!" He clumsily pointed to the ceiling. The four soldiers bounded through the house to the stairs and ran up to the roof, stumbling and knocking into each other in their haste.

Andrew followed them up and out onto the roof. He was fairly certain there was no fire; the soldiers must be mistaken. Or were they up to something? He silently watched as the men tore up the tin roofing and placed smoking rags underneath. They were setting a fire, not fighting it! As the men staggered back into the house, Andrew ducked into a darkened corner until they passed. He heard them leave the house noisily, exchanging quick words with the guard at the door.

"You have a lovely house!" one of them said to Josie on their way out, and the other men laughed.

Andrew crept out of his hiding place and heard crackling on the roof. He rushed to the bathroom to retrieve one of the buckets of water he'd stored there, then carefully crawled out the window onto the roof to douse the sparks the soldiers had planted.

"Andrew, do you hear that? Is that fire?" Josie shouted as she hurtled up the stairs.

"I'm seein' to it right now. Ain't nothing, Miss Josie!"

Josie went into a hallway closet to find another pail they could use, but there was nothing there. "Oh, Lord, help us!" She ran up the small staircase to the attic nook and searched for something, anything, to help fight the flames. Glancing out the large attic window, she gasped. The window provided a view of the whole town, and Josie could see the hellscape Columbia had become. It was one surging ocean of flame, more like the medieval pictures of hell she'd seen in books than her precious hometown.

"And *this* is civilized warfare!" she spat.

"Miss Josie!" Andrew yelled from the roof. "Miss Josie!"

Josie hurried down to the window where Andrew was tossing water. She took the bucket from him and refilled it with water from the bathroom, then rushed back to him.

"This is how the 'cultured' Yankee nation wars—upon women and children!" she muttered as she grabbed the bucket back from him again and hurried to the faucet. "This is how they must conquer!" She took the full bucket back, and Andrew doused the roof one last time, snuffing out the sparkling flames.

Andrew and Josie descended the stairs to the first floor, where they saw that another soldier had arrived and was talking to the guard by the back door. Josie strode directly up to the men.

"Mrs. LeConte, I'm very glad you are safe," Mr. Davis said.

"No thanks to your compatriots," she replied contemptuously. "If you'll excuse me, I need to reassure myself that my roof will survive your friends' protection." She strolled right past them and out to her back lawn. She peered up at the top of her house, searching the roof for sparks. Satisfied with that side of the house, she circled around to the front, shielding her face from the heat of the nearby flames. Andrew followed behind her, his bucket still in his hand.

Inside, Mr. Davis looked at the guard scornfully. Staring back at Davis nervously, the guard had no idea that the man in front of him was, in fact, not a fellow Yankee but a Confederate spy whose blood was boiling. An enemy in a brilliant blue disguise.

"No more men allowed in," Davis said. "If anyone tries to get in, deal with them." The guard nodded. Davis stepped out to the porch but turned back to the guard. "Remember, we protect this house. If it is fired, or molested in any way, I'll come looking for you." *And you have no idea how easy I'd find it to slit your Yankee throat,* he thought.

Mr. Davis stepped off the porch, disappearing into the swirls of smoke.

———◆———

Having lost McQueen during his trek through the streets, Dr. William Reynolds stepped into his yard just as the front door of his house flew open. A soldier stumbled out onto the porch, leaned over the railing, and vomited over the side. Flames shot up from the houses around his own, but miraculously his house had not yet caught fire. Reynolds could see a handful of soldiers stumbling around inside, opening drawers and throwing his family's possessions around. Trunks, drawers, and boxes were broken open, the contents scattered everywhere.

"What the devil do you think you're doing?" he bellowed angrily as he stormed in. "Get the hell out of my house!"

"Oh, is this your house?" one of the soldiers said, sauntering up to him with a deceptively friendly face. "I thought we'd found a right nice chicken coop." At this the soldiers laughed, and several circled the room, making chicken noises and strutting around like roosters as they carried on looting.

"Get out!" Dr. Reynolds snarled. "Get out of my house!" He picked up a broom leaning in the corner and swung it at the men, who were so drunk that they stumbled over each other as they laughed and jumped out of the way. He brought the broom down on a soldier's back, and the broom snapped in half. The delirious young man groaned, snatched the broken half of the broom from the floor, and whipped around. The young soldier pulled out his pistol, but Reynolds noticed that his hand was shaking. *Has he ever used that gun?*

"Hey!" Another Yankee popped his head inside the front door. "House next door has whole boxes of whiskey in the basement! Come on!"

Most of the soldiers rushed out of the Reynolds house, a few purposefully slamming against Dr. Reynolds on their way. But the young soldier remained where he was, pointing his gun at the doctor.

"You think you have a right to use your pistol on a man defending his property from vandals?" Reynolds said. "Then I guess you'll have to shoot." The young soldier, who looked no older than a schoolboy, trembled with anger and fear, struggling to keep his arm steady.

"Pete, come on!" one of the others shouted at him from outside. "You're thirsty, aren't ya?"

Dr. Reynolds could tell Pete had lost his nerve. After a few moments, he lowered his gun and dashed out.

Dr. Reynolds closed the door and surveyed the damage to his living room. Pictures were smashed, books were torn apart, clothing was strewn across the floors. Someone had taken the fire poker and dug into the walls, leaving the poker sticking out of the clock face on the floor like an arrow in a bull's-eye.

Outside the house McQueen approached the front porch, watching the delirious soldiers making their clumsy escape. He glowered at the Reynolds house and drew his pistol.

———•+•+•———

"Where is Bill?" Betty Reynolds shouted at Reverend Porter when he returned to the Miot house.

"He's gone back to your house," he said quietly, trying to appear calm.

"You let him go? Why did you let him go!"

"Betty, there was no stopping him, I'm sorry."

"He'll be back soon, honey, I'm sure of it," Magdalen said, putting her arm around Betty.

"He's got . . . an officer escorting him," Reverend Porter stammered.

"Oh, an officer! A Yankee officer!" Betty shouted. "Because we all know how helpful *they* are!"

As if on cue, a group of rowdy soldiers barreled into the house. Little Anna cried out, and Theodore picked her up, holding her tightly. The soldiers staggered around the room as if there was no one else there, picking items up and slamming them back down: a picture frame, a teacup, a vase. Some dashed into the dining room, sweeping all of the silver from the table. Others ran upstairs and broke open doors, locks, and drawers. "Get out!" Mrs. Miot screamed, seething as they fanned out into the house. The stomping on the floor sounded as if a hundred carpenters were at work. Soon scattered papers covered all the floors upstairs in the wake of the soldiers' search for money and valuables.

Two of the soldiers walked up to Mr. Miot. Without a word one of them seized his arms and held them behind his back as the other dug into his pockets and tried to wrest his watch and chain from him. Mr. Miot wriggled loose and pushed the men off of him. The men stumbled and fell on the floor, then laughed and joined their fellow soldiers in the kitchen, helping them carry out bags of flour, sugar, and rice, as well as containers of molasses and packs of bacon.

"It's not possible that you're going to take all of our provisions and leave us to starve," Mr. Miot shouted at the men, but they lurched toward the door, ignoring him. "Hey, I'm speaking to you!"

"Oh, don't cry, little Reb," one of the soldiers said, adopting a mocking Southern drawl. "We'll leave *y'all* some corn pone or whatever the hell *y'alls* eat." Mr. Miot and Reverend Porter followed them out onto the porch as they lumbered away, dropping a few bags of flour and sugar in the yard.

"Oh dear God, where's Bill?" a frantic Betty Reynolds cried. She ran to Porter, grabbing him by the shoulders. "He's lost, Anthony! Swallowed up by the inferno!" Magdalen helped peel her off the reverend, coaxing Betty back into the house.

"He'll be back, Betty. He'll be back."

"What if he's lost? Trapped . . . or worse . . ." Her lips quivered as she contemplated her own words.

"Mrs. Reynolds, please don't despair," Reverend Porter said. "The officer . . ." Betty turned to him contemptuously.

"The officer," she said with a scowl. The reverend was silent.

The women went back inside. Anna's cries had become hysterical hiccups as Theodore tried to calm her. Reverend Porter and Mr. Miot stood on the porch, watching the soldiers enter houses along the block as the flames, now only a block away, drew closer. Over the roar of the wind and flame, they heard the sound of cackling men jumping on a piano inside the house across the street.

"This violence cannot stand." Mr. Miot and Reverend Porter turned to see Miot's next-door neighbor emerge on the lawn with several other neighborhood men in tow. "They expect we won't fight back. We will."

"They've set fire to our city, ransacked our homes," said one of the men. "What will come next?"

"But how do you fight such a slippery mob?" Reverend Porter asked. "They're marinated in whiskey."

"We must stand our ground, protect our families," the next-door neighbor answered. "If any women or children in our care are attacked, that attacker must meet his death." The men around him nodded.

"I agree," Mr. Miot said. "Anthony?"

The men turned to the reverend, waiting for his answer. He paused, chilled by the certainty that this agreement would precipitate the shedding of blood, and the dread of the Yankee retaliation that would surely follow. But the men were right. He nodded his head.

"Yes. We simply must." Though he had never raised his hand against another man, Reverend Porter now felt prepared to do so.

"Anthony," Mr. Miot said, nudging his friend and pointing out into the yard. "Isn't that the officer you said was escorting Dr. Reynolds to his house?"

Reverend Porter looked at the dark figure approaching the house out of the twister of smoke behind him. He felt his heart sink into his gut as he realized it was indeed Lieutenant McQueen.

"Reverend Porter," the officer said as he came nearer. He had returned alone.

———•—•———

From her porch Emma strained to see Josie's house, unable to tell whether it was burning or not. She could see women and children huddled on the grass on the west side of South Carolina College, wrapped in blankets and shivering in the night air. All along the campus grounds, wounded soldiers stumbled to safety from the burning hospital buildings. Doctors and nurses fought the flames on the roof with buckets of water. Flakes of fire dotted the sky above the hospital, and the punishing wind carried flames from building to building. Around the gates surrounding the campus, Emma heard soldiers cursing and shouting.

It was a nightmare come to life. She couldn't have dreamed up anything more horrible. Her city had turned into a vision of hell, and it was closing in on her house and her family. And what of her father, her uncle, her cousin? Had they managed to get far enough away before the vast swaths of land circling the city were burned? Were they this moment jumping into rivers or futilely climbing trees to escape the flames?

Inside, Bessie and Sallie had collected bedding, clothing, and food to take into the back garden. Bessie held Carrie in her arms as Sallie passed boxes to Henry to carry outside. In the garden, he covered the boxes with a hastily ripped-up square of carpet to protect them from the sparks.

"Thank you, Henry," Bessie said when he returned. "I . . . don't know what else to do. We . . . can't be left homeless. What will we do about my precious Carrie?" Henry looked at Mary Ann, prompting her to take the baby from Bessie, who was shaking so vigorously now that she looked as if she might drop her.

"It's all right, sweet Carrie, you just hush up, now," Mary Ann cooed. "We gonna be all right." She carried the baby to a blanket on the floor of the living room and placed her gently down. Amazingly, amid the horror of her surroundings and the shaking in her mother's arms, Carrie was sound asleep.

"She's lost so much sleep on account of all that coughing," Mary Ann said. "Can't hardly believe she sleeping through this, though."

Emma opened the front door and stepped back in.

"The house will surely burn," she said with dispassionate certainty, as if she were predicting the sun would rise in the east tomorrow.

"Oh, now, Miss Emma," Mary Ann said, looking over at Bessie to make sure Emma hadn't set her mother off on another panic attack. "We just gonna pray that God gonna deliver us from the flames. Ain't that right, Henry?"

"Yes, ma'am." Henry nodded on his way up the stairs with water buckets. "But while we're waiting on the Lord," he continued under his breath, "I'm gonna go up and splash some water on the roof." But Bessie wasn't listening anyway. She was sitting on the floor, looking at Carrie, making swirls in the baby's hair as she slept. Mary Ann gathered shawls and blankets and wrapped them around Bessie.

Up on the roof Henry dumped buckets of water on the shingles and over the sides of the house to keep them wet. Downstairs, the women stood at the threshold of their home, waiting for it to catch fire.

Emma stood by the door, gazing out at the chaos. The wind howled outside and fiery embers hurtled through the air. The rumble of a building collapsing sounded nearby. "Our home will burn," she whispered.

At the Point of a Bayonet

Lieutenant McQueen hastened back to the Miot house and saw Reverend Porter talking to a few men on the front lawn.

"Reverend, Dr. Reynolds begs you to bring the ladies back," Lieutenant McQueen said as he approached, wiping his wet face on his sleeve. "We've saved the house, and the presence of the ladies will make it safer."

Reverend Porter narrowed his eyes suspiciously at McQueen. *How could it be safer for anyone back in the center of town?*

"What have you done with Dr. Reynolds?"

"Nothing, Reverend, he's at his house."

"Wait here," the reverend said, glaring at McQueen. He rushed inside to get his military shawl, a remnant of his time as an army chaplain. As he wrapped it around himself for protection from the flaming debris on the wind, he recalled the short conversation he'd had with the Union soldier who had issued the shawl to him.

"Don't mind wearing a Union cloth, do you?" the man had said, smiling.

"We're all human under these clothes, my boy," Reverend Porter had said in return. Now here he was, protecting himself from a fire set by Union soldiers with a shawl their own army had given him.

He struck out into the heart of the conflagration. He didn't believe the lieutenant; McQueen probably only wished to lure the ladies into the street so that he could help his fellow soldiers rob them.

"Reverend Porter?" McQueen called after him.

Porter headed north toward the Reynolds house, and as he approached the neighborhood, he stopped in his tracks. The entire block of houses where the Reynolds house stood was ablaze. The street was bright as day.

"Reverend Porter."

Porter whipped his head around, expecting to see McQueen behind him. But the man standing there was General Sherman, who had recognized the reverend from their conversation earlier in the afternoon. "A hideous scene," Sherman said, shaking his head.

When Porter realized he was looking at the very man who had promised him that the city of Columbia would be safe from harm, his eyes blazed with fury.

"Yes," he shouted, feeling his blood pulsing in his temples, "especially when you remember that women and children are your victims."

"No, no, Reverend," Sherman replied. "You are mistaken. Your governor is responsible for this."

"How is that?"

"Well, whoever heard of evacuating a place and leaving it full of liquor?" Sherman was angry too. "My men are drunk, and this is the cause of all this madness."

Reverend Porter had never wanted to strike another man before, so he was shocked at how powerfully that impulse seized him at this moment. *We are both seeing the same catastrophe unfold,* he thought. *And he wants to put the blame on us?*

"Why didn't your governor destroy all this liquor before he left? There was a very great quantity of whiskey in the town when we arrived."

"With respect, General," Reverend Porter responded, "I have seen sober men fire house after house."

Sherman appeared shocked at this news. Just then an officer rode up and saluted Sherman, who recognized him and said, "Captain, did I not order you that this should stop?"

"Yes, General, but the First Division are as drunk as the soldiers who came in yesterday morning."

"Then, sir, go and bring the Second Division and have this stopped. I hold you personally responsible for the immediate cessation of this riot." The captain passed on, and Sherman turned back to the reverend. "I did not order this, Reverend."

Reverend Porter looked out at the multiple infernos, the refugees in the street, and the rowdy soldiers issuing their primal screams. "And yet here it is, happening," he said.

Sherman moved on, and Reverend Porter headed back to the Miot house. As he hurried down the street, clutching his shawl tightly at the neck, a sergeant and two privates lurched toward him. The sergeant—his gait unsteady and his eyes glassy—approached the reverend, seized his shawl, and struck him violently on the left temple.

"What is a goddamn rebel doing with a Union shawl?"

On the porch the women at the LeConte house listened to the wind's fiery roar, punctuated by the sounds of houses collapsing only blocks away. Across the campus green, where scores of refugees and wounded soldiers huddled in terrified clusters, the hospital buildings had caught fire again on the north side.

"It's flaming again!" the women heard a male voice exclaim nearby. It was Dr. Thomson, standing in front of the house next door, looking at a patch of grass burning on the side of the main hospital dormitory. The wind spread the flames quickly to the shrubbery surrounding the hospital and then to the building itself.

Seeing the women on their porch, he ran over and, stumbling, caught himself on the railing. He had just come down from the roof of the hospital, where he and his fellow medics had been frantically fighting the spread of the flames. He was drenched with sweat and blackened by exposure to the smoke and soot.

"Ladies, could I trouble you for some water?"

"Oh, Dr. Thomson, of course!" Emma said, gesturing for Sallie to go inside and get the water. "You must come in and sit down."

"No time," he said, panting, trying to catch his breath. "Gotta get back over and help fight this thing. It's starting up again."

Sallie came back with a jar of water, followed by Mary Ann and Henry. Dr. Thomson grabbed the jar, sucked down the water in a few gulps, and wiped his face with his arm.

"Henry will go with you to help," Emma said. Dr. Thomson handed the jar back to Emma, and she passed it to a grim-faced Mary Ann. As she did, Henry stepped down the porch stairs.

"Yes, sir, I'll go with you."

"Henry, no!" Mary Ann snapped, to which Henry shot back a quick "Hush up, woman!" under his breath.

"We could use all the help we can get." Dr. Thomson sighed. "Come on with me then, boy."

The men set off across the campus to the smoldering hospital building. On the porch Mary Ann covered her face and fought back the tears she knew she would be scolded for showing. Her crying always irritated Emma most of all. But the LeConte women, standing there on the porch, paid no attention to Mary Ann. Their gazes were fixed on Dr. Thomson and Henry as the men receded from view.

"Hold up, boy," Dr. Thomson said to Henry, suddenly stopping and looking over at the guards at the campus gate about ten yards away, where four soldiers were standing guard. "We need to get us some more help." He strode quickly up to the gate, and Henry followed.

"Come and help fight this fire," Dr. Thomson demanded of the main guard, who looked back at him impassively.

"Would you see your own soldiers burned alive?" the doctor asked the guard angrily.

The guard didn't answer.

"I said, would you see your own Yankee soldiers burned alive by the fire your men have made? There are Yankees *and* Confederates trapped in there." Dr. Thomson was shaking with anger. "Your own men! Will you let them die?"

"I-I," the guard stammered, then turned to two of his men. "We'll follow."

Dr. Thomson nodded, and he and Henry took off for the hospital, which was now burning briskly, as the guard and his two men followed, leaving behind only one man to guard the gate.

A crowd of raucous soldiers quickly noticed the lightly guarded gate and descended, shouting and sneering at the lone soldier as they approached.

"We go in! The college buildings should burn like the rest of them!" One swore, hurling a bottle at the gate. Hearing the ruckus behind him, Dr. Thomson stopped at the entrance to the hospital.

"Boy," he said to Henry, "We've got to find an officer to stop those Yankees from coming in. If they push into campus, the hospital has no chance. They'll fire it up for sure. Follow me." Dr. Thomson yelled at the three guards to go up to the roof and start dousing the flames as he and Henry ran through the south entrance to the building, racing out the front door on the north side onto Pendleton Street. Chaos reigned and riot raged among officers and soldiers, civilians, and slaves. A squirming mass of people stretched along the avenue, and the newly arrived relief brigade that had been sent in was struggling to scatter it and get it under control.

A Yankee soldier gripped a young Columbian man's neck with both hands and, spitting and swearing, wrung it like a dishcloth as the two men rolled on the ground. An officer, pulling people away from them, screamed at the soldier to release the man, but the soldier, blind in his drunken rage, gripped the man's neck even tighter.

A shot rang out, sending the panicked crowd scurrying in all directions as soldiers and officers from the relief brigade rounded them up. Dr. Thomson and Henry struggled through the crowd and saw the Union soldier roll off of the other man and onto the street, the left side of his lifeless face a bloody pulp.

Dr. Thomson and Henry broke from the crush of people and ducked behind a tree. They backed farther away from the mad rabble until they reached Sumter Street, where they saw

General Sherman talking to a newly arrived fireman and his group of volunteers.

"General!" Dr. Thomson shouted. Sherman turned around.

"We need a guard for the campus grounds now," Dr. Thomson continued. "The hospital is under siege and it's already fired." He pointed down the street to where the soldiers were starting to climb the gate.

"General Oliver!" Sherman bellowed, and an officer on the edge of the crowd came running.

"Round up those offenders," Sherman commanded, pointing at the growing throng by the gate. Oliver whistled to a group of his men helping to round up the rioters and waved them to follow him. Oliver rushed to the campus gate and fired his rifle into the air. Soldiers jumped off the gate at the sound, and Oliver's men seized them.

Mr. Davis darted away from the crowd, holstering his smoking rifle as he ran down Pendleton Street. He'd just shot a Union soldier dead in the heat of the riot—the first time he'd taken a man's life outside battle.

He wondered if, tonight, it would be the last time.

———————

Reverend Porter staggered on the street, reeling from the sergeant's blow to his head. A kaleidoscope of orange light swirled before his eyes as he fell to the pavement. The dark figure that had struck him slowly came into focus, and when he could see the sneering face above him, he leaped up and fell upon the man, wrestling him to the ground.

"Stop! Reverend, no!" one of the privates yelled, moving to break up the fight.

Reverend Porter held the sergeant in a headlock from behind while the sergeant's hand stretched to reach his holster.

"He's got a gun, and he's off his head drunk!" the private shouted, trying to grab the reverend's arm to pull him off the sergeant. "We can't answer for what he might do!"

The private lost his grip on Reverend Porter and fell to the ground, leaving the two men lurching sideways like one massive body.

Seeing out of the corner of his eye that the sergeant was struggling to unholster his gun, Reverend Porter let go and jumped back, giving up the contest. He slumped down onto the street with his aching head in his hands while the sergeant grabbed the shawl, wrapped it around himself, and stalked away with his mates in triumph.

Reverend Porter breathed heavily, his head throbbing, blood trickling down his face. The roar of the wind and the human howling swirled around him, giving voice to his dizzy anger and fear.

"Sir! Sir!"

Reverend Porter looked up, and before him stood another soldier, reaching out his hand to assist him. Bleeding from the temple, the reverend weakly held out his hand, and the soldier lifted him to his feet.

"Sir, I saw that man strike you and rob you of your shawl. It is an outrage."

Reverend Porter, still breathless from his fight, just shook his head in agony.

The soldier lowered his gun from his shoulder. "I'm Officer White, and I'm ashamed this night to admit that I belong to this army. If you'll hold my blanket and knapsack, I'll get that shawl for you."

Reverend Porter nodded as White then dropped both items at his feet, and, gripping his bayonet, stormed off in pursuit of the sergeant. He met a fellow officer on his way who joined him, and, spying the sergeant lumbering down the road, still flanked by the two privates, they sped up and seized the man.

"Back off!" White shouted at the two privates, whipping his bayonet around and pointing it alternately at each of them as his partner held the sergeant. The privates slunk off, and White turned to the sergeant, held tightly by White's comrade.

"That's a nice shawl, buddy!" White spat at him. "I believe I know where you got it from, you little cockroach!" The man struggled against the other officer but was unable to break free. "Now, I think we're going to take a little trip, my friend."

The men marched the sergeant back to where Reverend Porter stood, White keeping his bayonet tipped toward the sergeant as they moved. Watching the men marching toward him, Reverend Porter's eyes widened, and he wiped the blood trickling down the side of his face.

"Apologize to that gentleman for striking him," White yelled, "and give him back his shawl!"

The sergeant stumbled forward and clumsily removed the shawl. "Sir, I—I," he mumbled, "I am sorry for the offense."

"I think you can do better than that!" White shouted.

"I'm terribly sorry, Reverend!" the sergeant stammered. "The devil must have taken possession of me. . . . I don't deserve your forgiveness but I . . . I heartily ask for it!"

Officer White nodded, and the sergeant then bowed his head and handed the shawl to Reverend Porter.

"I accept your apology," Reverend Porter said, taking the shawl.

Officer White nodded at his partner. "Get him to the guardhouse."

The two men departed, and Reverend Porter, overwhelmed by Officer White's bravery, got out his pocket Bible to write down the man's name.

"Please, officer," he said, "let me know your name."

"Sir, I'm Ron White." He looked around at the chaos in the streets and at the flames being carried on the wind in all directions. "I enlisted to fight to preserve this union. I did not come here to burn down houses or insult women and strike unarmed men." He placed a hand on the reverend's shoulder. "If I was a Southern man, as you are, in the sight of this burned city, I would never lay down my arms while I had an arm to raise."

———•◦•———

Dr. Thomson and Henry dashed through the first floor of the hospital. They passed through a large, dimly lit dormitory full of wounded soldiers. Men missing arms and legs, their bodies covered in blood- and pus-soaked bandages, hobbled and crawled around the room, looking for a way to escape the smoldering building. A few nurses scurried around the room, trying to help the men out of the building, but there were too many patients to help, and the nurses were too small to carry the full weight of the amputee soldiers. The wounded men's moans filled the hall as they made their way to the windows and doors. Henry stopped cold when he saw a legless man crawling on his arms across the floor in front of him, trailing a dark glaze of blood in his wake.

Henry grabbed the man under the arms and carried him over to an open window. He shouted to a soldier who had just landed outside on the grass. "Take him, sir! Can you please take him?" After he eased the wounded man out the window, Henry looked back for others to help.

"Let's go, boy!" Dr. Thomson called from the end of the hall. "No time!"

"I be right behind you, sir!" Henry shouted back. Dr. Thomson nodded and disappeared up the staircase.

Henry saw another soldier, arms wrapped in bloody bandages, struggling to swing his bloated and gangrenous legs off of his cot. Henry ran over and knelt down beside him.

"Lift your arms, sir," Henry said. The soldier raised his bandaged hands and Henry grabbed him around the waist and lifted him up off the cot. The man's feet slid onto the floor, and at this he wailed, collapsing back onto the cot. As the man continued to howl in pain, Henry bent at the knees, took the man's arms over his shoulders, and lifted him up. He lumbered over to the window with the wailing man on his back and bent to set him down on the sill.

"Help!" Henry shouted from the window. "Help, please!" Outside, wounded soldiers limped and crawled around the campus green, consumed with their own misery. Seeing no other choice, Henry crawled through the first-floor window and jumped outside onto the grass, then grabbed the screaming soldier and pulled him through. The man landed on his rotting feet, emitting a shriek that cut through the roar of the wind. Undeterred, Henry took the man onto his back and carried him to a nearby tree, bent down, and, unable to hold the weight any longer, tumbled onto the ground. As they rolled, the soldier's screaming suddenly stopped.

Henry disentangled himself, then lowered his head close to the man's face. He felt a slight breath on his cheek—the man was still alive.

Henry looked up at the roof, where he saw Dr. Thomson amid a small group of doctors and nurses tossing buckets of water over the side. He also saw that small fires had cropped up in the shrubbery that ringed the hospital, and the wind had carried some of the flames onto the side of the building itself. He had to get up to the roof.

Henry pulled his overshirt off, folded it up, and placed it under the soldier's head. He then dashed back into the hospital and up to the roof, on the way passing doctors and nurses running up and down the steps, carrying full buckets of water on the way up and empty ones on the way down. Among them were the captain who had been guarding the campus gate and his two privates.

"Here, boy, take this!" one of them shouted to Henry, handing him a full and dripping bucket. Henry took it and leaped up the last flight of stairs to the roof, where he found Dr. Thomson directing five of his hospital colleagues where to toss water.

"Boy!" Dr. Thomson shouted at Henry. "Over here."

Henry rushed over to the edge of the roof where Dr. Thomson stood and looked down onto Pendleton Street, where he had seen the rioting so recently.

Trails of fire coiled up the building toward the roof, pushed skyward by the maniacal wind.

Reverend Porter trudged back to the Miot house, once again wrapped in his shawl. As he approached the gate he saw Lieutenant McQueen rushing toward him.

"Where have you been?" McQueen shouted. "I have taken the ladies home, and your wife is miserable without you."

"What! You've taken my wife and children back to that burning house?" His eyes blazed with anger.

"No, sir!" McQueen answered, raising his voice. "The house is saved. Your wife's hand was slightly burned, and your little daughter fainted on getting back. But they are now safe, and Mrs. Porter is almost distracted with the uncertainty regarding your fate."

"Lies!" Reverend Porter bellowed. "I myself just saw the Reynolds house in flames! Yes, burning like an inferno!"

"I . . . I . . ."

"So where have you taken my family? Delivered them over to some of your villainous compatriots, no doubt!"

"Reverend Porter, you are mistak—"

"You have taken all that is dearest to me somewhere, I know not where!"

"You're wrong, they are—"

"I swear to almighty God, you little snake," Reverend Porter screamed, "if there's been foul play, either your life or mine is near its end!"

McQueen, shocked by the reverend's escalating anger, took a step backward.

"And with God on my side," Reverend Porter continued, "I will not go first!"

THE DEVIL'S OWN

IN THE EARLY MORNING THE camp in the woods was still dark when Joseph heard the measured *tramp, tramp* of troops marching nearby. He joined John and Johnnie, who were already crouched down by last night's extinguished campfire, looking through the clumps of trees to see a regiment pass along the road within a hundred and fifty yards. They all drew a long breath.

The sound of the footsteps receded, and a nervous tension settled on the camp as the dawn emerged. Joseph opened his mouth to speak—he was worried about the wagons they had left hidden only about fifty yards from where the soldiers had just passed. Suddenly a sharp cry of "Look out!" broke the stillness of the morning air.

Sandy rushed to the campfire from the nearby slave camp. "That's Captain Green who said, 'Look out!'"

Joseph leaped up and ran for the wagons. If the soldiers were looking for them, they would surely venture into the woods from the road. And the first location they would come to was the hiding place for the wagons. Worse, he had carelessly left his pistol in one of the wagons, as well as a satchel containing money, jewelry, railroad bonds, and a notebook of lecture notes. All the valuables he had brought from Columbia were now ripe for pillaging by soldiers who were hell-bent on looting all they could.

He crept through the foliage to the first wagon and found it unmolested. Crouching behind a wagon wheel, he could see all the other wagons.

"Damn," he cursed under his breath. Yankees were swarming another wagon. Joseph was no more than ten feet away, but he had no hope of saving anything. He dropped to his hands and knees, crept back into the thicket, and at a distance of thirty yards watched the soldiers knock trunks and boxes to pieces and rummage through their contents in the early morning light. Some of the men fanned out to search for the owners of the wagon train. Fearing discovery, Joseph decided to shift his position; with the foraging Yankees between him and the encampment, the only option was to move farther away from camp. This meant there was no way he'd be able to reach the others to warn them. He crossed the main road and, his head low to the ground, heard the sounds of the Yankee pillage continuing just a few yards away.

———

Henry raced back and forth between the roof and the washroom on the topmost floor of the hospital. He swung two empty buckets on the trip down and then lugged them, full and dripping, back up to the roof. Teetering at the edge, he doused the sides of the building with water to put out the flames. Dr. Thomson barked out orders of where to go with the buckets, while the three Yankee soldiers flung water over the side of the building, directly onto the steaming roof. The doctors and nurses, having fought hospital fires for hours, had in the early morning light switched their attention back to their patients, who were now scattered on the hospital grounds and along the campus green.

Henry crossed to the campus side of the roof to see if he could get a view of the LeConte house. Sure enough, there was Emma on the porch, gazing with her pale, sad face at the horrifying tableau before her: wounded soldiers, both Confederate and Yankee, covered the green, as did women and children who, after fleeing their burned houses, had sought refuge from the marauding soldiers on the well-guarded campus. The air was quieter now; the cacophony of rioting was dissipating and the gale-force winds had slowed.

"Sir," Henry said to Dr. Thomson as he strolled to the staircase, "I be needing to go check on Miss Emma and them."

"Okay, boy, you done a good lot of help," Dr. Thomson said. "God willing, we may have got this blaze under control."

Exhausted, Henry slunk down the hospital steps. Though the new day was dawning, the air was thick with a grim red murkiness. Through the early morning haze he caught sight of the tree where he had left the soldier with the gangrenous feet. He staggered over and knelt down, leaning in to get a closer look at the young man. His eyes were closed, Henry's work shirt was still folded underneath his head, and his puffy face was a sickly blue.

He was dead.

———— ·◆· ————

Lieutenant McQueen calmly shook his head at Reverend Porter.

"Reverend, please take a breath and follow me." McQueen turned and headed toward the Reynolds's neighborhood, hoping that putting some distance between them would help defuse the reverend's anger. After going a few yards, he turned back and waved the reverend on.

"Please, Reverend Porter."

The reverend, frozen in his rage for so long, finally took a step, and they rounded Washington Street together. To Reverend Porter's shock, there stood the Reynolds house, standing tall and evidently unharmed amid the crumbling and still smoking remains of the other houses around it. Along with the Baptist church, it was the only building left standing in more than ten blocks.

Reverend Porter stood spellbound, utterly mystified, remembering the moment when he'd seen the Reynolds house shot through with raging flames.

"But . . . this is incredible," he mumbled. "I'm sure I saw the house burning like it was the devil's own. The whole street was aflame!"

"It was dark, Reverend Porter," McQueen offered. "Fires were burning everywhere. I'm sure you were just . . . confused."

Reverend Porter quickly extended his hand.

"Lieutenant, I have judged you unjustly. I ask of God and of you your forgiveness. I took you for a villain, and now I find I am under great obligation to you."

Lieutenant McQueen took Reverend Porter's hand and shook it warmly.

"Forgive you, certainly, Reverend. I knew by your face what you felt, and it's perfectly natural after this night's experience. I imagine you have the worst opinion of every member of this army. But you must know, Reverend, we are not all like this— there are many gentlemen and Christians among us."

As small fires still burned on the side of the road, the men slowly made their way down Washington Street until they came to the lonely house, standing amid the apocalyptic ruins of the neighborhood.

As Lieutenant McQueen helped soldiers and neighbors clear away debris in the road in front of the Reynolds house, Reverend Porter stepped onto the porch and entered the house.

Meanwhile, a tiny flame flickered on the roof.

———————

Emma sat on the steps of her porch, looking out on the campus green at the multitude of patients who had escaped the hospital during the night. Some were attempting to return indoors, crawling on the ground or calling out to the nurses for help. Others lay eerily motionless on the ground. The Yankee soldiers who had tried to attack the campus were tied to each other on the ground outside the campus gates, their bodies twisted into various awkward positions. Emma stood and trudged back inside.

Sallie lay sleeping on the sofa in the living room, and Bessie stood over her, whispering in her ear. In a few moments Sallie opened her eyes and stretched her arms toward her mother.

"Oh, is it already day?" she said. "I'm so glad. I thought the light in the window was the reflection from a fire."

Emma went directly to the washroom to clean her face, which was filthy from soot, dirt, and sweat. She watched the grime coagulate in the sink and slowly drain down. Patting her face dry, she felt as if she'd just awakened from a frightful dream. She looked into the mirror and was surprised by what she saw—she hadn't slept in days and half expected to see a haggard old woman staring back at her. But even after the nightmare of the past twenty-four hours, the face she saw was somehow the same young girl who had so recently kissed her beloved father good-bye and promised to take care of her mother and sisters . . . the same girl who had so delighted in the company of her cousin Johnnie when he visited the house back in January, and who had sung her favorite song "Aura Lee" to her sick baby sister while rocking her to sleep just a few days ago. This long war had finally come to her doorstep, and, after a night of hellfire, she was still here—exhausted but, even now, fearless. In the kitchen her mother and sister sat quietly, shell-shocked. Bessie held Carrie in her lap, carefully spooning another dosage of syrup and powder into the baby's mouth. A worried-looking Mary Ann served bread and butter, though no one could eat.

The front door opened and Henry entered, shivering.

"Henry!" Mary Ann hollered as she ran over and hugged him tightly.

"Calm down, woman," he whispered, eyeing the LeConte women as they approached. "We ain't at home."

"Oh, I was so *worried*, Henry! I saw you up there with the buckets and the water and the fireballs. Thought you was gonna trip and fly away on the wind!"

"Well," Henry said, nodding to Emma, Bessie, and Sallie, "the fires over at the hospital ain't no more trouble. I reckon we pour enough water on that building to sail a ship on. And the wind ain't doin' nothing no more."

"Henry, you've been so faithful," Emma said. "Thank you." Hesitantly placing her hand on his arm, she felt the coldness of his skin. She looked directly into his eyes, and said, "Thank you, Henry."

Henry nodded. "Yes, ma'am." He held her gaze for a moment, nodded, then dropped his eyes to the floor.

"You talk to any Yankees, Henry?" Mary Ann asked. "'Bout what they plans are?"

"Don't rightly know. I talked to some men up on the roof that was helping, but we . . . mostly talk about fire 'n' water."

"I suspect they're not done with us yet, the devils." Emma smirked. She took crying Baby Carrie out of her mother's arms and sniffed at her diaper. "Probably time to give her a change," she said, leaving the room and striding up the stairs.

A knock came at the door. Mary Ann brushed passed Henry to answer it. She swung open the door, and there was Aunt Josie, her face smeared with coal dust. She stared at Mary Ann with the dead eyes of a ghost.

———•◦•———

Crouched in a clump of saplings near the main road, Joseph was in constant danger of discovery by passing Yankee soldiers. He couldn't believe how many there were. They'd already pillaged one of the wagons, and there was no telling what state the other wagons were in now. He had to try to get back and see if there was anything left to save. He crawled back toward the wagons and saw a tall Yankee coming straight toward him. Joseph quickly dropped flat to the ground on his stomach and gingerly turned onto his back. *This is it*, he thought.

The Yankee was just a few feet away when he laid down his gun, adjusted his rucksack, drank some water from his canteen, and leaned against a tree. Joseph's heart raced, and it was all he could do to control his breath. He laid his head quietly down on the pine straw and closed his eyes, praying for a miracle. He kept his eyes shut tight, terrified that if he opened them he would find himself staring death in the face. He heard a rustle, a sigh, and then, to his amazement, retreating footsteps. He opened his eyes: the Yankee had passed on.

Joseph sat up and looked all around for signs of other approaching soldiers. There was no one. He rose slowly to his feet and crept out of the woods, then quickly recrossed the road and regained the main wood. He crept cautiously toward the wagons on his hands and knees, trying to fix his mind on anything but the destruction of his family's valuables and his own manuscripts.

How well I've trained for this exercise while duck hunting, he thought as he crawled. *But now I'm the duck!*

About thirty yards from the camp, he heard the murmurs of Yankees and slaves talking in low voices. *Who are those Negroes?* Were they the Niter Bureau slaves? He'd had doubts about their trustworthiness from the beginning—now he cursed himself for the foolish decision to allow their families to come along on the trip. What was to keep them from fleeing from the wagon train and joining a Yankee faction whenever the opportunity presented itself? Though he couldn't hear what they were saying, there could be only one reason for Yankees to talk to Negroes: information.

Sure enough, he heard one of the Yankees say his and John's names and then an angry Yankee voice yelled out.

"We'll beat every bush, but we'll find them."

Creeping nearer, he saw a second party of soldiers pile the trunks and boxes that had so recently been rifled through back onto the wagons. One of the men pulled a small object out of his jacket. Joseph held his breath. The soldier lit several matches and tossed them onto the wagons, which contained everything of value Joseph and John owned. The wagons caught fire, and columns of smoke shot upward. Joseph shut his eyes tightly as the crackling and roaring of the flames filled his ears. He felt as if he'd been kicked in the stomach. Opening his eyes again after a few minutes, he looked at the blaze. All was turning to ash.

Bessie and Josie hugged as if they hadn't seen each other in years, and for some seconds no one could speak.

"Oh, Josie," Bessie said as they moved to the back piazza. "Your house . . . is it gone?"

Josie shook her head, smearing the soot on her face as she wiped tears from her eyes. "No, it was saved. Oh, it burned, yes. Mightily, several times. The damned thing kept catching fire all night. But we managed to smother it in enough water to keep it from spreading too quickly."

"Oh, thank the Lord."

"That Mr. Davis was especially helpful."

"Mr. Davis!" Bessie gasped. "He . . . helped you?"

"Oh, yes, and he was rather nasty to the other guards for being so slow to fight the fire."

A crashing sound came from the kitchen. Bessie rolled her eyes and shook her head. "Mary Ann. That poor thing is a mess—doesn't know which way is up. Mary Ann! Get out here, girl!" A few moments later Mary Ann quietly entered through the back door, her eyes wet from weeping and her face slack with worry. She looked up and, shocked to see Josie there, swallowed her tears.

"Miss Bessie," she began, her voice barely above a whisper.

Bessie frowned.

"Mary Ann, now what on earth is wrong with you?"

Mary Ann jerked her head up and dropped her hands down to her apron.

"Them Yankees, Miss Bessie," she murmured, "they gonna make Henry go off with them."

Bessie had never heard Mary Ann sound so delicate. But she was in no mood to play the sympathetic listener. She looked at Josie and scowled. "I just don't know, Mary Ann."

"I think they gonna," Mary Ann whispered, nodding her head slowly. "And I'll have to go with him."

Bessie pursed her lips. It was very possible that all the slaves would go. She knew that the field Negroes wanted to leave with the Yankees. But Mary Ann was different, Bessie thought. She'd come to them as an orphan, and Bessie and Joseph had taken the place of her father and mother. Emma and Sallie were like her sisters.

"He don't wanna go, no he don't," Mary Ann said. "Unless they drag him away, he'll never leave." She took a deep breath, rubbed her hands on her apron, and moved to the door.

"If I have to go," she said, her lips quivering as she wiped tears from her eyes, "I can still cook two more meals for the family." She disappeared inside.

"I don't know what to do about the slaves," Bessie muttered after Mary Ann left. "We'll lose them all, I suppose."

Up in the drawing room, Emma looked out the window at her mother and aunt talking on the piazza below. She'd given Carrie another dose of powder and syrup, and the baby was now dozing on her shoulder. She looked out at the smoke rising from the devastated city, her hatred smoldering.

Are they done with us yet? Or resting up now to visit us later with even greater terrors?

She looked down at Carrie and kissed her forehead.

As she looked back out the window, an explosion sounded nearby, shaking the house.

On the western side of Columbia, smoke rose from the blackened bank of the Congaree River, which was covered with exploded shells. Small flames licked at the grass and drifted toward the dozens of bloodied Yankee corpses strewn about the riverbank.

Watching the grisly scene, Mr. Davis smiled. He could hardly believe how well the plan he'd suggested to the retreating Confederates had worked.

"Miserable Yanks didn't even see it coming," he whispered. Digging his heels into his horse's side, he went galloping back into the center of town.

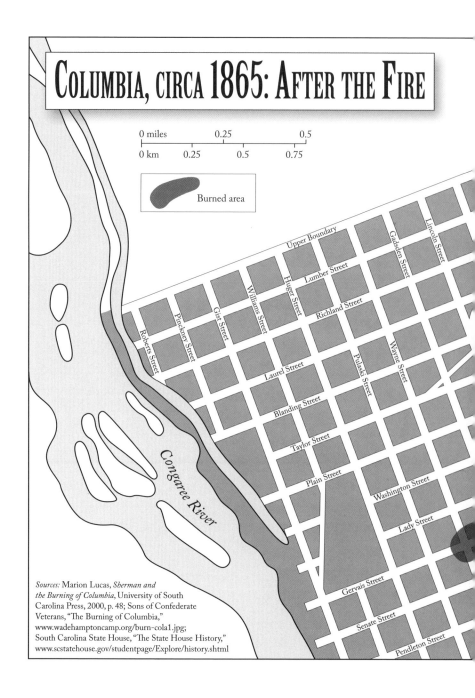

COLUMBIA, CIRCA 1865: AFTER THE FIRE

0 miles   0.25   0.5

0 km   0.25   0.5   0.75

Burned area

Upper Boundary

Lincoln Street

Gadsden Street

Lumber Street

Huger Street

Williams Street

Richland Street

Gist Street

Pinckney Street

Roberts Street

Wayne Street

Pulaski Street

Laurel Street

Blanding Street

Taylor Street

Plain Street

Congaree River

Washington Street

Lady Street

Gervais Street

Senate Street

Pendleton Street

Sources: Marion Lucas, *Sherman and the Burning of Columbia*, University of South Carolina Press, 2000, p. 48; Sons of Confederate Veterans, "The Burning of Columbia," www.wadehamptoncamp.org/burn-cola1.jpg; South Carolina State House, "The State House History," www.scstatehouse.gov/studentpage/Explore/history.shtml

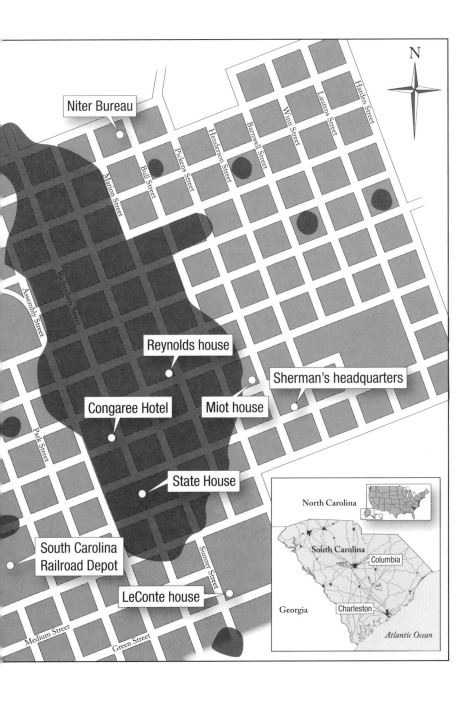

Niter Bureau

Reynolds house

Sherman's headquarters

Congaree Hotel

Miot house

State House

South Carolina
Railroad Depot

LeConte house

North Carolina

South Carolina

Columbia

Georgia

Charleston

Atlantic Ocean

EVERY BIT GONE

AT THE REYNOLDS HOUSE THE living room looked as if it had been picked up and shaken: boxes, drawers, and trunks had been broken open and their contents scattered across the room by the marauding soldiers from the night before. Expecting new horrors to materialize any second, the Reynolds and Porter families huddled in the center of the room, having heard the explosion echo across the neighborhood and unsure which direction it came from. Anna, who had been napping in Theodore's lap on the couch, leaped up and screamed when the blast hit.

"Oh, precious Lord, what could be happening now?" Magdalen mumbled, close to tears. "Is it a new attack?"

"Why on earth would there be a new attack?" Dr. Reynolds exclaimed. "What remains to attack?"

"Fire!" Lieutenant McQueen yelled from the front porch. Reverend Porter rushed outside.

"Reverend, I've just seen flames on the roof," McQueen said. "I thought we'd finished it off, but it looks like this fire's not done with us yet."

"Was the house shelled?"

But Lieutenant McQueen was already off, recruiting neighbors and soldiers who had been clearing debris from the street to help fight the fire.

"Everyone out!" Reverend Porter bellowed. Within a few minutes Dr. and Mrs. Reynolds, Magdalen, Theodore, and little Anna were standing on the lawn, staring up at the large flames glimmering and gyrating on the roof.

"Mommy, what was the boom-boom?" Anna asked between sobs. Magdalen looked down at her with no answer ready.

"Mama doesn't know, Annie," Theodore said, grabbing his sister's hand. "It was over by the river, anyway."

The people in the yard formed a line stretching into the house and up the stairs, passing water from the well between them. Lieutenant McQueen and a few fellow soldiers ran up to the roof carrying buckets of water and wet towels. As they doused the flames as a team, McQueen looked west and saw the dead bodies along the riverbank. Turning northward, he saw the smoldering arsenal building uptown, smoke rolling up from its devastated ruins.

"When does it end?" he muttered.

⸻ ◆ ⸻

Joseph crept from his hiding place and moved toward the camp. He reached the hollow and peered out from behind a tree. Several Yankees were wandering around the camp, and there was no sign of John, Johnnie, Captain Green, or any of the slaves. His heart sank. *Did they flee? Have they been taken?*

He scampered back to his hiding place, lest he be spotted. He waited a few hours, chewing on leaves to keep his hunger at bay, until he couldn't contain his anxiety over the others anymore. At sundown, seeing a fire burning at camp, he decided to risk it again. He crouched down and crept through the woods, the light of the campfire filling his watery eyes as he pressed forward. On the edge of the woods he could see no one near the fire—yet there it was, burning brightly. Were the Yankees there? At the sight of the flames he couldn't help but think of food. His stomach rumbled. Taking a deep breath, he decided to chance it. He crept out of the thicket and moved haltingly toward the campfire.

The camp appeared to be empty. Shivering, he leaned toward the fire, stretching out his hands to receive its warmth. He heard a rustling and footsteps—he whipped around and saw a little slave boy, about eight years old, approaching him. He didn't know his name, as he was from the Niter Bureau families.

"Where are Sandy and Charles?" Joseph asked the boy.

"They all up where the wagon been," he said.

"Go tell them I'm here."

The boy crept away. The sky was dimmer now, and a chill breeze wafted through the trees. As he watched the boy go, Joseph feared that even his own slaves might have already crossed over and were talking to the enemy. Realizing he might be moments away from being seized, he stepped back into the bushes and crouched down to observe. His stomach growled as he waited for what felt like an eternity for any sign of movement. Finally, twenty minutes later, he heard footsteps crackling over dead leaves on the ground. Seeing no Yankees, he stepped out of the bushes.

"Master, I so glad to see you safe!" Sandy said as he and Charles approached.

"Where's John?" Joseph asked.

"Oh," Sandy said, "them Yankees take Mas' John and Mas' Johnnie right off with them!"

"Great God! Why didn't they run?"

"I dunno, sir, I dunno. Mas' John coulda got away easy, but he walk right up to the Yankee, and the Yankee put he gun right to he chest and he gives himself right up."

"Because of Johnnie?" Johnnie had been sick, after all, and John may have thought it better to surrender than to risk his son's illness relapsing.

"I suspect—yes, sir, I reckon so," Sandy mumbled.

"And where is Captain Green?"

"Dunno, but think he must be in the woods some way."

In the woods some way, Joseph repeated to himself. What was Sandy hiding?

"Have you got anything to eat? I'm famished."

"I put away some meat and bread for you," Charles said in his deep baritone, and he handed Joseph pieces of boiled pork and some rough cornbread. Taking the food, Joseph greedily stuffed pieces into his mouth. As he ate he watched as more slaves returned from the woods. Looking around, he noticed that two of his slaves were not among the assembled. What was going on?

"Why, where are my house boys?"

"Them Yankees take them and Mas' John's three boys with them to ride the mule. They beg to stay but the Yankees make 'em go."

Joseph licked his fingers and wiped his mouth with his arm.

"Them Yankees wanted to take all us men," Charles said, "but we begged to stay to take care of the womens and childrens."

Joseph felt panic overtake him as the daylight grew dimmer and dimmer. Here he was, surrounded by slaves, some of which, he was sure, were conspiring to turn him and Captain Green over to the Yankees.

"And the property in the wagons?"

"All gone—every bit gone," Charles said. "They took the silver, jewelry, and clothing with them; the rest they burn up with the wagons."

"Tell me, Charles," Joseph began, "do you think we are being hunted? Are these Yankees still out there, looking for me?" *Will he even tell me the truth?*

"Honest, sir? I think you in danger."

Feeling vulnerable in the bright light of the campfire, Joseph backed away.

"I'm going to go a little way into the woods for some shut-eye," he told Charles and Sandy, and he pointed out the area where he would hide. "If Captain Green returns, come find me."

———————

"How's it feel to tie up your own soldiers, treatin' us like damn graybacks?" A bound Yankee soldier shouted at one of the guards at the campus gate.

"Feels all right," the guard responded. He'd grown tired of answering the insults of the fellow soldiers now in his charge. A hundred restless Yankees were huddled on the ground outside the gate. In the wake of their recent rioting, they were under guard, with their hands tied behind their backs. They struggled against each other, shoved, spat, and argued as the darkness grew thicker.

Emma listened to the soldiers hollering insults and threats. Walking among them as one of the guards, wielding his pistol with apparent glee, was Mr. Davis.

"Miss Emma," Henry said as he loped up to the porch from the hospital, where he'd been talking to Dr. Thomson, "you doing all right?"

"I suppose so." Emma looked down at her shoes, avoiding Henry's eyes. She didn't even know how to act toward Henry and Mary Ann anymore. They still seemed willing to do as she told them, but there was no denying that life had changed.

"That explosion," Henry began, "Dr. Thomson say it was owing to shells up by the river, buried by Confederates when they leave. Some Yankees try to dig 'em out, and one went off accidentally. Then . . ." He mimicked the explosive chain reaction with his hands. "Pop! Pop! Pop! Pop! Poppowpow!"

"And what of the Yankees who were digging them out?" Emma asked.

"They dead, ma'am. Many of 'em, dead."

A flash of a smile stole across Emma's face.

"Well," she said with a note of triumph in her voice, "that's poetic."

"What's poetic, ma'am?"

"Our men got a few Yankee scalps after all. And without even being here to do it."

Henry looked away, unable to respond. Suddenly the distant racket of the quarreling soldiers was pierced by the squeal of an animal approaching the LeConte property.

Emma and Henry tried to follow the sound—it was coming from the backyard. Emma ran inside, and Henry ran around the house and saw that a small number of soldiers had broken open the door to his slave quarters and were inside tossing around clothes and furniture, looking for valuables. Meanwhile, a large pig circled the yard, its squeals growing louder and louder as three soldiers, one with a bayonet and the other two with knives, tried to corner it.

"Henry!" Mary Ann called from the kitchen window. "Get back! They crazy!"

Henry dodged both the pig and the soldiers, backing away to lean against the side of the house. He knew what was coming: he'd heard stories of hungry soldiers on Sherman's march stalking and cutting up whatever livestock they came upon. Though he could barely keep track of what he was seeing in the darkness, he could hear everything: the sound of the soldiers wrestling the pig to the ground, the animal's squeal morphing into a blood-curdling howl, the *swish* of a knife being frantically, repeatedly driven into flesh. The pig's screams were matched by Mary Ann's and Emma's. Less than a minute later, the soldiers had finished their grim work and stumbled away with the newly acquired pig meat wrapped in a towel.

Henry leaned against the side of the house, his eyes wide, his breath short and labored, as if he himself had partaken in the butchery. He slid down to a crouch, placing his head in his hands.

Mary Ann stepped out the back door holding the lantern up to look at the pig on the lawn. She screamed at the sight of the massacred animal, its legs splayed and innards drenched in blood. She covered her mouth as tears sprung from her eyes.

"Henry," Mary Ann sniffed trying to pull herself together, "you ain't hurt, is you?"

"Naw," Henry said. "Just . . . not ready for what I seen. And for sure not ready for *that*." Henry pointed at their ransacked quarters, then looked at his wife—she was shaking. "Well, what is it, girl? They gone, they ain't botherin' us no more."

"I heard somethin', Henry. I should tell you."

"Well, what is it?"

"Heard one of the soldiers outside the gate said it."

"What *is* it, Mary Ann?" Henry hissed.

She took a step closer. "He swore that the campus buildings will burn tonight."

Joseph knelt in the woods and prayed. He hadn't been to church in a long time and had never been much inclined to seek divine intervention. Alone in the dark, with his brother and nephew kidnapped, Captain Green having disappeared, and his own slaves possibly conspiring against him, he had nowhere else to turn. So he bowed his head like Bessie always demanded everyone do during the dinner prayers, and asked God for deliverance.

As he mouthed his silent plea, he heard the familiar crackle of footsteps on leaves and pine straw.

"Who's there?" he whispered.

"Master Joseph?" It was Charles, holding a lantern.

"I'm here," Joseph said, standing up from his crouch.

"Captain Green's returned."

"Where is he?"

"In the woods up there." Charles pointed in the direction of the burned wagons.

Joseph took a step, then halted suddenly. *Is this a trick? Is he sending me into Yankee hands?* But he couldn't stop himself, desperate as he was for an ally. He moved farther into the woods. The scent of burned wood reached his nose, and he tried to follow it, creeping through the blackness. He wanted to whisper Captain Green's name, but he feared discovery by the Yankees who might be lying in wait for him.

Joseph turned around and around, trying to get a glimpse of the captain, losing hope that this was anything but a ruse to get him captured. All was silent. He started whistling— a long, low whistle—but there was no answer. He whistled again a little louder, blowing out all of the breath in his lungs. Silence again. He looked around, trying to discern any shapes or figures in the darkness—had the world ever been as dark as it was now?

A low, whirring whistle issued from the shadows.

Joseph stumbled in the direction of the whistle, then stopped and listened. Had he gone the wrong way? The whistle now sounded distant. He whistled again. A few seconds later, a short, feeble whistle answered back. He then heard the crushing of dry leaves under cautious footsteps. Soon the rustling stopped. He couldn't stay silent any longer.

"Captain!" he whispered. No answer. He called again a little louder. Nothing. He pushed ahead until he stood beside an enormous oak tree. He called again.

A few moments later, a craggy whisper. But he couldn't make out what it said.

"Captain! Captain?"

"It is I," Captain Green replied hoarsely. "Joseph?"

"The very one!" He felt around in the darkness near the tree. "Why are you so hard to find?" Both men moved around the tree, finally clasping hands.

"Oh, Captain Green," Joseph said excitedly in a hushed tone, "what a relief to see you alive! I thought I'd lost you!"

"No, not just yet," Captain Green whispered. "Give this old man a hand, will you?"

They set out for the campfire, Captain Green limping and leaning heavily on Joseph.

"I'm afraid I'm not much good to you right now, Joseph," the captain said.

"We need to get you some water; you're surely dehydrated."

"Yes, water would be good. I wouldn't turn down a steak and some roasted potatoes, either. Got that handy?" The captain's chortle turned into a wheeze.

"Pardon," he said. "Been lying in that clump of saplings all day, not moving a muscle. Was almost discovered, but . . ." Captain Green was suddenly silent.

"What is it, Captain?"

"I heard them talking . . . the Yankees. They were talking to a Negro . . . it was a Negro that tipped them off about us being in the woods."

"One of ours?"

"Can't be sure."

They reached the campfire, which Charles was stoking. The other LeConte slaves sat on the ground in silence. Out of the darkness, Sandy came running toward them from his perch on the edge of the woods, where he'd been on lookout.

"Master Joseph, some men coming this way!"

Joseph, Captain Green, Sandy, and Charles all backed away from the light of the campfire, keeping their gazes fixed in the direction of the incoming footsteps. Shadows danced in the treetops as a small group emerged from the woods and into the clearing. It was the Niter Bureau slaves.

———

Henry and Mary Ann wandered across the green in the chilly night. Armed guards were posted along the brick wall that circled the campus. The refugee women and children who had sought sanctuary within the campus gates had been taken in by other families, and the wounded soldiers who had covered the lawn had been taken back to the hospital over the course of the day.

But not all the patients had been able to return to their beds. The grass was strewn with bodies covered by sheets. More than twenty patients had died—from fright, exposure, or both—after escaping the burning hospital into the freezing early morning. The doctors and nurses had been too busy treating the wounded inside all day, able to take enough time only to lay sheets over the stiff, ice-cold corpses.

"They ain't burning these buildings, they just trying to scare us." Henry bent down next to a body and lifted its exposed hand off the ground, placing it snuggly under the sheet.

"I don't know, Henry. Probably wouldn't believe them if'n they said they *won't* burn 'em. Can't trust what they say."

They came upon the tree where Henry had left the dying Yankee soldier early that morning. Henry knelt down next to him.

"This a Yankee soldier, Mary Ann. Carried him out here myself."

"He with the Lord now."

"Hope so." Henry gazed at the ghostly figures on the ground. "Better than this place."

Henry stood up and put his arm around Mary Ann as they strode back to the LeConte house, where Emma sat on the porch talking to Mr. Davis in a hushed tone.

"Mr. Davis says they won't be burning the buildings," Emma said as Henry and Mary Ann stepped onto the porch.

Henry nodded uneasily, noticing the dark expression on Mr. Davis's face.

"No, they won't be burning anything else," Davis said. "But they'll be looking for *you*, Henry."

Henry and Mary Ann exchanged suspicious looks.

"There's talk of rounding up Negro males to leave with them tomorrow."

10

BONES PICKED CLEAN

JOSEPH AND CAPTAIN GREEN'S HEAVY footsteps sounded against
the frozen ground as they trudged back toward Columbia. They
had left their encampment under cover of night with nothing
more than the clothes on their back. Joseph wore his overcoat
and Captain Green, who had lost his coat while out in the
woods, wore a blanket that he'd fashioned into a hooded cloak
with the help of a piece of twine. Flames rose from houses
on both sides, and, as the men cut through the darkness, one
house's roof gave way, and the clatter of the collapse echoed
through the night.

They had had no choice but to flee back to Columbia.
Come sunup the Yankees would be searching every square
foot of those woods. So Joseph and the captain had decided
to escape while the darkness could hide them. Joseph paid
Sandy twenty dollars to take his other slaves and John's back
home, and Charles, the leader of the Niter Bureau slaves, one
hundred dollars to see that those belonging to the bureau
were returned safely.

"Take care of yourself," Sandy had said when they parted. "I hope the Lord will keep you from them Yankees!"

Sandy's friendly tone echoed in Joseph's head as he cut a path through the brittle cold. Was it Sandy's voice that Captain Green had heard, ratting them out to the Yankees?

"I surely never expected to see any of the slaves again," he said.

"It is odd," the captain said. "Negroes can walk the streets with no fear of capture. Or, at least, fewer fears than fugitives like us."

"How the world has been turned on its head," Joseph said.

Joseph couldn't escape thoughts of what terrors his brother and nephew might be experiencing right now. It had probably been foolish to bring young Johnnie along, sick as he was. Now the two of them were probably chained up in some prison somewhere, being starved or beaten or . . . worse.

The men heard light footsteps close behind them in the darkness and turned to see a well-dressed young black man almost treading on their heels.

"What's the meaning of this?" Joseph hissed. He abruptly whipped around to address the man. "Why are you following us so closely?"

"I'm sure sorry, sir," the young man said. "Guess I'm right eager to get home." He smiled brightly. "My house is just up yonder on the hill." He pointed toward a house brilliantly lit by a fire on the hearth about two hundred yards from the road.

"There Yankees up there in that house?" Joseph asked.

"Naw, sir, should be nobody but colored folks."

"Yankees trouble you much?"

"Lawd, yes, sir, very bad all day. I afraid they maybe come back tonight."

"Well, good night," Joseph said, eager for the man to pass on.

"Good night, sir." Joseph and the captain watched as the man passed on through a gateway and scampered up to his house.

"That boy could very well inform on us," Joseph whispered. "We best move along quickly."

The men hurried ahead and had just arrived at an embankment, when they heard the clatter of hooves galloping away from the house of the man they'd just talked to. Their impulses quickened by days of dodging and hiding from Yankees, the men instantly jumped over the zigzag fence that bordered the road. Just as they folded themselves into a corner of the fence, twenty Yankee cavalrymen dashed by so close that their horses' heels struck the rails the men hid behind. The cavalrymen passed on, and Joseph crawled over to where Captain Green was hunched.

"Captain, what should we do? They're no doubt looking for us."

"Sit tight."

"But what if they . . ."

The men's whispering was drowned out by the thunderous *clump-clump* of the cavalrymen returning from their search of the long embankment. Joseph sprang back over to his part of the fence and lay facedown on the dirt. Instead of passing on, this time they stopped right in front of where the men were hiding. They proceeded to rein up their horses, and some dismounted. Joseph's heart beat ferociously in his chest.

"Didn't see a thing," one of them said.

Now we are lost, Joseph thought.

The road was muddy, so many of the men strode over to the grass to lean against the fence. Horrified, Joseph lifted his head to see that one of the soldiers was standing so close that he could have grabbed his legs. Only the darkness kept him from being seen.

"We'll just wait it out. We got time. Hell, we got all night. They can't hide forever. And they're here somewhere."

"Well, LeConte and Green can't get far. They have no horses."

Joseph watched as the soldier shifted his weight against the fence and spit. A dip of soggy tobacco slapped against the ground and splashed onto Joseph's cheek.

———— ·◆·◆·◆· ————

Early in the morning, two corps of soldiers marched by on Sumter Street with their immense wagon trains. Bessie, Sallie, and Emma stood on the porch, staring out as the guards who had been positioned all over the campus left their stations to join their comrades. With the memories of the inferno that swallowed Columbia still fresh, the ladies watched angrily as the men prepared to leave town unpunished.

"The last of the armies are leaving the city, it seems," Josie said as she stepped onto the porch. "The provost guard has broken up camp, too." She stared out at the campus green, now cleared of the corpses that had covered the lawn yesterday.

"They've picked our bones clean and now it's on to the next Confederate body, I suppose," Emma said bitterly. "And they'll leave our open wounds to the stragglers. But at least they helped clear the bodies off the green, so I suppose we should be grateful."

"I hate to say it," Bessie said, "but I wish they would stay another day or two. There's no telling what villains are out there waiting for the armies to leave."

The LeConte women watched the wagon trains begin their slow march out of town.

The remains of Richardson Street

"Uncanny, isn't it, to see them leaving in such a disciplined fashion," Emma remarked. "You'd never know they'd lifted a finger against the city at all. So well behaved they are now." The train moved through town to a chorus of hisses and boos, which brought a smile to Emma's face. "These Yankee monsters know what they've done, though. And so do we."

The women watched as some of their own slaves joined the wagon train. But Mary Ann and Henry were not among them.

"Well, at least Henry is still with us," Bessie said.

"For the time being," Emma interjected. "I can't watch this anymore." Emma shuffled inside, and the other women followed her into the house.

At that very moment Henry stood in the backyard with a shovel, digging a grave for the pig carcass that lay gutted on the grass. Henry had already taken his knife and stripped the body of most of its meat so that all that was left of the poor animal was its bones, guts, and head. The pig's eyes hung open, and it seemed to be staring at Henry as he dug. Henry paused after every few shovelfuls, unable to stop himself from looking over at the animal's seemingly watchful eyes.

He finally marched over to the pig and closed its eyelids. "Ain't no reason for you to be so nosy," he mumbled. "You just rest, now."

Henry dragged the pig over to the hole, let it fall in, and tossed dirt onto the carcass. Turning to refill his shovel with dirt, he caught sight of a Yankee soldier ambling onto the LeContes' front lawn. Henry immediately dropped to his stomach, flat on the ground.

The soldier strode up to the front porch. He walked the length of it, looking off both the east and west railings to see around the sides of the house. From the living room window, Mary Ann watched as he strode back to the porch steps, descended, and angled for the backyard. She bolted through the house and out the back door.

"Henry!" she whispered, stepping out onto the back piazza. But Henry was already crawling on his belly back to the slave quarters at the far end of the yard. He rushed in and locked the door behind him. Mary Ann, seeing the soldier emerge onto the back lawn, scuttled down the piazza steps.

"May I help you, sir?" she said, scurrying toward him. She eyed the shovel sticking out of the ground a few yards away from where they stood.

"Just looking for your boy," he said. "Need him to come with me—we'll soon be moving on."

"Mary Ann, what does this man want?" Bessie called, stepping down from the piazza onto the back lawn.

"Miss Bessie," Mary Ann cried, "he lookin' for Henry."

"Yes," the soldier said, "and I do believe I saw him go in there." He pointed to the door to the slave quarters. Listening from behind the door, Henry swallowed his breath.

The soldier stepped forward, and Bessie rushed to block his path.

"Would you have him go against his will?" she blurted out.

In the kitchen, Emma stood at the window, watching her mother arguing with the soldier. *What does that snake want?* A robust knock sounded at the front door. Emma recognized the knock—it had to be Mr. Davis.

"Please come in," she said, opening the door. Davis stepped inside, holding a small box. He was still dressed in Yankee blue. "We're having some trouble out in the backyard," Emma told him.

They crossed to the back of the house and out to the piazza, where Bessie was standing her ground as the soldier tried to inch closer to the slave quarters.

"I wish to see your boy, Henry," the soldier said. "He may not want to see me, but that's no concern of mine."

"If you don't get off of my property, I'll send for the guard," Bessie snarled, her anger rising in her throat.

"I myself am a guard, ma'am. I don't think that will do you much good."

"Well, there are two officers at my sister's house, and I will send for them. What do you think of that?"

The guard caught sight of Emma and Mr. Davis on the piazza, looking at him.

"Best get back to the wagon train," Davis said to him. The soldier, visibly spooked by the sight of Davis, turned and left the yard.

"Thank you ever so much, Mr. Davis." Bessie sighed, watching the soldier go.

"It seems you scarcely needed my help, Mrs. LeConte," he replied. "But I'm happy I was here to assist." He then turned to Emma and handed her the box.

"What is this, Mr. Davis?"

"Our army is going, Miss LeConte," he said. "Please, this is for you." Emma opened the box to see a bouquet of ribbons and feathers sitting atop a torn piece of red cloth the size of her own hand, burned on the edges and curling up. It was part of the South Carolina flag that had been flying at the State House. "That's all that's left," Davis said. "I'm sorry I couldn't do more for Columbia."

"Mr. Davis, can't you stay in the city at least another day?" Bessie pleaded. "With no guards, we're bound to be the targets of stragglers and deserters. God only knows how poor Joseph is faring. No telling when he'll return . . ."

"I'm sorry, Mrs. LeConte, but I can't stay," Davis said. "I have to go where the Union army goes, though my heart is with the Confederates."

Bessie's face fell.

"You've still got your loyal Henry," he continued. "He'll not let anything happen to you."

"If he wants to leave there's no stopping him," Bessie said.

"He's still hiding in the slave quarters." Mr. Davis laughed. "I don't think he's going anywhere."

Bessie tried to smile.

"In the coming weeks, if the Yankees enter your house, I shall certainly be with them. Be sure you do not betray me by recognition."

He bowed to Bessie and Emma, then departed the LeConte house in silence.

———•◦•———

In the cold, gray dawn, Captain Green wheezed and limped as he struggled to keep up with Joseph, who was hurrying onward down the road. They were trying to put as much distance as possible between themselves and the cavalrymen, lest the men decided to take another ride.

Burrowed behind the fence for more than half an hour, they had stayed perfectly still while the soldiers had loitered nearby, chewing their tobacco, kicking the dirt, and vowing to find "those damn rebel skunks."

Finally, at long last, the men remounted their horses and rode away. By the feeble light of a thin crescent moon, Joseph grabbed the fence and pulled himself to a crouch, then crawled over to the captain, who appeared as a dark gray bundle of rags. When Joseph poked him with a stick, the captain rose up with glazed eyes as if in a trance. He swung his arm in the air like a blind man. Realizing that the captain probably didn't even have the strength to pull himself up, Joseph reached out his hand, gripped the captain's flailing limb, and pulled him up, eventually having to put an arm around the captain's waist to steady him on his feet.

The men crept down the embankment and stumbled into the freezing, knee-deep water of the river. As they waded across, the captain moaned, and Joseph swore he could hear the man's bones creaking.

The two fugitives hurried to the other side of the river, cut through the overgrowth by the water, and emerged onto a dirt road. The captain, exhausted and shivering, stopped to catch his breath. The air had become bitterly cold. Joseph worried about keeping up their speed, but he also knew the captain, who had only one healthy lung, wouldn't be able to manage with no breaks. So he paced back and forth, stamped his feet, swung his arms, and struck his chest to keep warm while waiting for his friend to regain his strength.

"Joseph," the captain said, "I can't go any farther. You must leave me."

"No, Captain, I won't. Here, take my arm—I'll help you up the hill."

The men proceeded up the incline, the captain wheezing and coughing the whole way. He couldn't walk more than three hundred yards without stopping to rest. Ahead of him Joseph stumbled in his eagerness to outrun the Yankees. After the sun rose, the popping of Yankee guns sounded in the distance, and columns of smoke from burning homesteads rose on all sides.

Dear God, we're surrounded, Joseph thought.

The remains of Columbia's jail

After they had gone only a mile, he heard what sounded like horse hooves on the road behind him. In a panic he whipped around and saw that Captain Green had collapsed onto a pile of rails by the roadside.

"Captain! Captain!" Joseph yelled, running back to his friend.

"It's no use, Joseph," the captain mumbled. "I can go no farther." He struggled to lift his head. When he opened his eyes, his pupils rolled around beneath fluttering eyelids.

Joseph looked around to see if there was anyone on the road behind them, friend or foe. The captain moaned as his dry, cracked lips tried to form words. He rolled over onto his side and exhaled a slow, labored breath. Then there was silence.

Fearing the worst, Joseph leaned down to listen for the captain's breathing. Feeling a very slight wisp of air against his cheek, Joseph lowered his head to listen to his friend's heart: it was still beating.

"Captain, just wait here. I'll go get help."

Fearing he had little time, Joseph ran as fast as he could down the road. He heard a rooster crow and followed the sound through a gate that he hoped would lead to a farmhouse. He ran at full speed for half a mile before finally reaching the house, the grounds of which were overgrown and, the rooster having apparently given up, perfectly silent.

"Hello! Hello! *Hello!*" He yelled louder each time, and soon a giant pit bull terrier was bounding toward him, barking furiously. Joseph backed away and darted his eyes around, looking for something to use as a weapon. The dog slowed, taking a few steps at a time as he continued to growl and snarl.

"Bingo! Bingo, you better git!" A slave girl holding a half-eaten apple appeared and moved fearlessly toward the dog, who whined and scuttled up to her. She saw Joseph peering at her from behind an oak tree in the yard but didn't say a word to him.

"Please, girl, let me see your master or mistress. It's an emergency! I'm a Confederate officer!" *Should I have told her that?*

She took a bite of her apple and, with a full mouth, shouted, "Miss Millie! You got a visitor!" The girl then moved around the side of the farmhouse, the dog following closely on.

The front door opened narrowly, and the ghastly, terror-stricken face of an old woman stared out at Joseph.

"Please, ma'am, I need help with my friend, an officer in the Confederate army!"

The woman's face twitched as she nervously looked around to see if Joseph had brought any stragglers to her home. Her hands shook even as they gripped the side of the door. She pulled the door open wider and gestured for Joseph to come inside.

"Please, ma'am, may I bring him here? He just needs a place to rest and recoup, and if you have any food . . ."

"Sure enough, you can bring 'im here," the woman said. "We ain't got much, but what we got is yours."

Joseph nodded and turned to run and get the captain, when the woman's voice stopped him.

"A few Yankees came by yesterday, threatening to return today to clean us out," she said. "Fact is, we been waiting for them every moment, expectin' they would be devils enough to hit us in the mornin'. We thought you was an advance guard—my husband ran out the back door like a flash when he heard the dog barkin'."

"I do apologize for the scare," Joseph said.

"Anyway," the woman continued, "I reckon you best get your friend here and quick."

Joseph took off running. As he sped back toward the main road, he whipped his head all around, looking out for Yankees that might have followed him, listening for horse hooves and the sounds of rifles being locked. Passing through the gate where he had first heard the roosters, he wondered how he was going to get Green back to the farmhouse when he reached him. Would he have to carry him on his back? Perhaps, if the captain was strong enough to stand, he could coax him to the house with the promise of food?

But all these questions evaporated when he reached the main road.

The captain was gone.

FOSSILS AND ASHES

AT THE REYNOLDS' HOUSE REVEREND Porter stood in the front yard holding Anna in his arms while Theodore ran out to the street to get a better view of the retreating troops. Theodore moved his gaze from the wagon train to the surrounding piles of ashes, crumbled chimneys, mounds of jagged concrete, gutted houses, and collapsed brick walls. Every house on Washington Street for blocks and blocks had been burned to the ground. Smoke still filled the air and rose from the ground as if the very earth were roiling with anger over the assault.

Theodore turned his eyes back to the wagon train, and they fell on the figure of Lieutenant McQueen, who was strolling back up to the house.

"Hey, sergeant!" McQueen said. "Wanna help me stand guard?"

The Yankees had arrived in Columbia amid the booming of cannon fire, but they left in a silence that covered the city like a

Richardson (now Main) Street after the fire, as viewed from the State House

blanket. There was no shrill whistle of engines, no daily mail, no paper with news from outside the city. It was as if an entire town were suddenly stricken with a fiery curse and, when the smoke had cleared, reemerged as a ghostly, apocalyptic desert.

Emma and Bessie finally decided to leave the house and see what damage the fires had wrought. As they staggered like sleepwalkers through the city, they realized for the first time the extent of the devastation.

"Mother, it looks like we were lucky not to be burned out of house and home," Emma remarked as they stepped through the ruins in the center of town.

"Bessie! Bessie!" a neighborhood woman shouted, dashing up. "I heard about Josie's house, and poor Andrew!"

"What did you hear, Melody?" Bessie asked fearfully.

Melody paused. "Oh, dear Lord, have you not talked to Josie?"

"Yes, Melody, I have talked to her. What did you hear?"

"Well, I heard tell that Josie's house came crashing down and that her house slave, Andrew, perished. Just horrific . . ."

"Melody, you silly girl, that's just a complete fiction. Now you just go and tell the person who told you that that they should keep their wild stories to themselves."

"What on earth are we to do about these stories, Mother?" Emma said as an embarrassed Melody skulked away. "Poor Father and Uncle John and Cousin Johnnie . . . what if these terrible rumors reach them?"

Bessie had no answer and didn't appear even to be listening. She simply gazed wordlessly out at the city, which lay in ruins before her. The entire heart of Columbia was in ashes—only the outer edges remained. On the whole length of Sumter Street north of the campus, only one brick house was standing. The center of town was nothing but heaps of trash, scorched debris, tall bleak chimneys, and shattered brick walls. As they strolled through the northern end of Richardson, they saw a firefighter weeping silently as he sat on brick stairs, the only piece of his house that was left.

Richardson Street was in ashes. The stores, merchants, customers, wagons—everything that gave the thoroughfare life—had vanished. The shops were now graves of charcoal dust. Homeless refugees picked their way through piles of rubbish, brick, and timbers. The wind moaned through the lonely chimneys and whistled through the windows of the hotels and warehouses lining the street. The central market was a gaping wound, a ruined shell supported by crumbling arches. Its spire had collapsed, taking with it the town clock, whose shattered face now lay amid the rubble.

"It is even worse than I thought," Emma whispered.

They passed the old State House on their return home, and Emma paused to gaze on its corpse. Only the foundations and chimneys of the majestic structure were left. Emma recalled the grand bazaar that was held there only one short month ago; beautiful crafts and pieces of art were sold to raise money for their boys fighting the more numerous and better-equipped Yankees. The halls had been elaborately decorated, and her fellow Columbians had turned out in droves to take part in the festivities. She and Bessie had knitted little tobacco pouches, and they had sold all of them. Now, only weeks later, the building was no more than a fossil.

"Before they came here I thought I hated them as much as was possible," Emma said darkly. "Now I know there are no limits to the feeling of hatred."

The women finally reached their home, their hearts heavy. Even the sun didn't seem to shine as brightly, as if weakened by the sight of so much desolation. Emma sank into the couch in the living room, her face twitching with anger and sadness. She tried to block out the sound of her mother weeping in the kitchen, when suddenly she heard a commotion out in the backyard.

"Oh my precious Lord!" Bessie shouted from the kitchen before bounding out the back door.

"Mother, what is it?" Emma pulled herself up from the sofa and hurried onto the back veranda. "Oh great God!"

Into the middle of the backyard strode Sandy, leading all the other slaves who had gone with Joseph.

"Miss Emma!" Mary Ann rushed up to her. "The Yankees has caught 'em. Mas' Johnnie's back at home, and Master John's took prisoner!"

Joseph spun around, looking for any sign of Captain Green on or off the road. He rushed up to the pile of rails where the captain had been and saw a set of boot prints in the dirt. It appeared the captain had somehow regained his footing and started following Joseph. The tracks led away from the rails and back onto the main road. Green had clearly fallen down a few times—some of the boot tracks were obscured by far larger smudges that could only have been made by Captain Green's fallen body. The tracks led up the road in the direction he'd just come from.

But how did I miss him coming back? Joseph wondered.

Joseph started jogging back, following the tracks in the dirt. When he came to the gated lane he had taken up to the farmhouse, he saw that the boot prints continued on the main road. Realizing the captain must be straight ahead, Joseph sprinted up the road for a few hundred yards until he reached the summit of a small hill and saw a figure veering off the road at the bottom, heading toward another farmhouse.

Joseph sprinted toward his friend. "Captain!" he whispered as he closed in on him. The captain turned around and Joseph overtook him.

"Joseph," he said weakly, "where are we? Where did you go?"

"I thought you were done for," Joseph said. "I went to get help." Joseph looked the captain up and down. He looked like he'd been wrestling with a tiger: his pants were torn at the knees, and blood and mud were caked on his skin.

"Are you able to go on, Captain?" By way of answering, Captain Green started moving again, forging ahead up the road as rain started falling, quickly escalating into a downpour. Amazed at his friend's resurgence, Joseph quickly caught up with him.

As rain fell from the gray sky, the men veered off the road to take a shortcut through the woods. They crept through the forest and could see that the woods and pine thickets had been searched recently by the Yankees: horse and wagon tracks were everywhere, and the bushes and trees were plucked clean of fruit.

They continued on through the woods, up and down hills and across streams. Five miles farther along, Captain Green slowed down again, his tall, spare form swaying unsteadily. Finally, when they came to the other side of a thigh-deep stream, the captain collapsed on the bank.

"Captain?" Joseph, standing at the top of the bank, slid down to where his friend lay in the mud. Captain Green's face was sickly pale, his lips were purple, and his breath was raspy.

The Catholic convent in Columbia, reduced to rubble

"Captain?"

"Leave me," the captain whispered.

"Don't be ridiculous. Look—there's a house up there. Surely they'll take us in."

"Could be Yankees hiding there," the captain murmured.

"We'll have to take that chance." Joseph hopped up, ran to the house, and, pausing for the briefest of moments, knocked at the door. Inside he heard people scuttling around and laughing. He closed his eyes, exhaled a soft prayer, and waited for the door to open.

———

Once the last wagon train trailed off, silence settled over the neighborhood. Lieutenant McQueen had insisted on staying to guard the house from any renegade stragglers who might arrive now that their fellow Yankees had gone. He'd remained out in the front yard all morning, clearing it of debris and rubbish with young Theodore's help.

"Lieutenant, we can't thank you enough for your loyalty," Reverend Porter had said as he walked outside to check on recovery efforts. "I worry, though, for your safety. Your army has been gone for some time, and . . . I fear you could be shot if Confederate scouts meet you riding alone. I think you should go."

"Don't you worry about me," McQueen had said, refusing to move from his perch on a slab of concrete in the yard, where he sat cleaning his boots. "I can't leave knowing that your house is vulnerable."

"But, Lieutenant, if you stay, there are men enough in town to make you their prisoner. The town is angry . . . I fear you may become a target of their rage."

McQueen looked up from his task and saw that the reverend's face was serious.

"I'd pledge my life to see you safely returned to your lines," Reverend Porter continued. "If you stay, I think it will give you trouble hereafter."

"I understand your concern," McQueen said. "But it's not . . . morally honorable for me to leave."

"Nor is it morally honorable for me to allow you to stay." Reverend Porter smiled at McQueen, and the lieutenant nodded. He stood, his cleaned-up boots in his hands.

"Well, I guess I'll need to put these on then. All right if I clean up inside?"

A half hour later, the Reynolds and Porter families gathered around Lieutenant McQueen to say good-bye. He kissed little Anna and shook hands with Theodore. Betty Reynolds handed him a sack of biscuits, cornbread, and cooked bacon. Reverend Porter walked out with him to his horse to say a final farewell. As McQueen mounted his horse, Reverend Porter handed him a golden cigar box that Magdalen had given him one Christmas.

"Please accept this, Lieutenant. As a token of remembrance. Magdalen and I wish for you to have it."

McQueen held it in his hand for a moment and said, handing it back to the reverend, "Tell her I thank her, but . . . given what's happened here, no one would believe that a Southern man *gave* me a gold cigar box in Columbia. I never could convince anyone I hadn't stolen it."

"I see." Reverend Porter sighed. Then his eyes brightened. "Won't be a moment," he said, dashing inside.

Running into the house, Reverend Porter hastily wrote a letter addressed to General Wade Hampton or "any other Confederate into whose hands Lieutenant John McQueen might fall," detailing McQueen's noble conduct during the fire and his defense of the reverend's family. He signed his name in full.

"Keep this about you," he said, handing it to McQueen. "It may be of service during an emergency. Any Confederate should know that you are not an enemy, no matter what uniform you wear."

McQueen took the letter, folded it with a smile, and slipped it into his coat pocket. He then saluted Reverend Porter, tapped his horse with his heel, and rode away.

Watching McQueen go, the reverend breathed a silent prayer for him and returned to the house to begin the work of barricading it against raiders.

———◆———

Inside a house six miles away from Columbia, a fire burned in the hearth. Sitting before it in a crisp, clean shirt, white stockings, slippers, and a cotton dressing gown, Captain Green rocked in a chair, holding a pipe in his hand, enveloped in spirals of blue smoke.

"Ah, Joseph," he said with a sigh, his weakened voice barely there, "isn't this glorious?"

Behind the captain, three men and a woman sat at a table. Joseph stood watching the captain and nodding.

"Yes, it sure looks glorious," Joseph answered his friend. He turned to the table of people, two of whom were fellow refugees making their way back home. The owners of the house, Mr. and Mrs. Jones, stood up, and Mrs. Jones began to clear the table of the plates and leftover food and drink from the meal they had just consumed.

"Captain Green must surely stay overnight to regain his strength," Mr. Jones said to Joseph.

"Yes," Joseph said, "I think that's best. I really must return today, though. With many thanks for your hospitality!"

Joseph bid his hosts, friends, and Captain Green farewell. Before leaving, he knelt down beside the captain, who was now dozing in his chair, his head encircled with a halo of tobacco smoke.

"Shall I tell your wife and daughter that you will be with them tomorrow, Captain?" Joseph asked. Opening his eyes just a sliver, without changing his position, the captain replied, "Yes, yes. Tell them . . . tomorrow."

———————

The setting sun cast a golden light over the smoking ruins of Columbia. At the LeConte house, Emma, Sallie, Bessie, and Mrs. Green sat with Johnnie and Josie in the living room. Mary Ann brought in a pot of tea and began pouring. Sandy stood against the wall, his head bowed.

"Uncle Joseph and Captain Green were in the woods when they found us," Johnnie said, his hands trembling as he recounted his story. "They'd been gone all day, keeping an eye out for Yankees. But the Yankees found us anyway."

"What about your father?" Josie cried. "Did they hurt him?"

"No, ma'am. The Yanks who took us treated us right kindly. At least, compared to how your Yanks treated Columbia. I think Father'll be paroled soon."

"And Joseph?" Bessie asked, flinching at the prospect of a painful answer.

More ruins of Columbia

"He must have been captured," Johnnie said flatly, without looking up. "I don't see how he couldn't be. The woods were alive with Yankees."

Tears sprang from Bessie's eyes. Emma stepped to the window.

"I don't see how they could escape," Johnnie continued. "They probably would fare far worse for trying."

"Johnnie," Josie scolded, "why do you say that?"

"Even if they did somehow escape, the country was so entirely swept . . . I don't see how they'd be able to find anything to eat."

"This is dreadful." Emma sighed. "Just dreadful." Sallie, her eyes red with tears, stood from the table and wrapped her arms around her sister.

"If we at least knew that they were captured," Emma continued, "it would be less awful than the thought of Father hiding in the woods, cold and hungry, with the possibility of being shot."

A silence descended on the room. In the corner Sandy raised his head.

"Miss Emma, now don't you be worryin' none," he said brightly. "Them Yankees never catch Mister Joseph. That certain sure."

"The wagons are gone," Johnnie murmured.

"The wagons?" Emma said, turning around. With all the thought of Joseph, she had forgotten about the family's valuables he had taken with him.

"Everything was burst open. They took all the silver and valuables, slashed the clothing and linen with bayonets, took all the books and blankets, burned whatever was left, along with the wagons. They made a right mess of all our stuff. There ain't nothing left."

Josie and Bessie broke down and wept. Emma, not wanting to be seen crying, drew back and slumped down at the bottom of the staircase. She felt as if her heart were breaking. Mary Ann, seeing Emma's distress, padded over and placed a hand on her mistress's shoulder.

"Poor Miss Emma," she said. Emma looked up at Mary Ann, teardrops running down her face. Here was her house slave, bending down, pitying *her*. It was too much for her to take. She ran up the stairs and flung herself onto her bed. Her eyes tightly shut, she still couldn't escape the image of wild, roaring flames closing in on her.

Mary Ann walked out to the back piazza. Henry was outside cleaning up the lawn and trying to tidy up the grave he had dug for the pig, flattening the dirt with the back of his shovel. He sat down on a tree stump as Mary Ann sauntered up to him.

"What we doing, Henry?"

"We workin'."

"Uh-huh."

"We prayin'."

"What you gettin' at, Henry?"

"We livin'." He stood up, looked around him, and leaned in to give Mary Ann a kiss. "Just like before, but . . ."

Mary Ann watched her husband closely as he paused to put his thoughts together.

"Like before, but . . . plenty different."

"Better?" Mary Ann asked, "Or worse?"

"Dunno," Henry admitted. But as he reached out to move a stray hair off his wife's face, he smiled. "Guess we's all gonna find out."

———•—•———

Under the dim light of the crescent moon, Joseph LeConte entered Columbia at the extreme northern end and walked a mile and a half down the length of Richardson Street, struggling to believe what his eyes showed him. The fire cut a path five or six blocks wide right through the center of the city, leaving only the eastern and western edges untouched. Not a house was standing and the streets were deserted.

Tall chimneys stood skeletal and ghostlike; lonely brick walls held up nothing, their vacant windows like eyeless sockets. Surrounded by this nightmare of desolation, he quickened his step until he was sprinting down the street, panicked and desperate for a glimpse of the brick wall surrounding the college campus that would tell him his house was safe.

So this is what we fought for, he thought. *Four years of blood spilled and now . . . all is ashes.*

He arrived at the ruins of the State House—now just a confusion of fallen bricks, charred wood, and mortar—and stopped. Diagonally across from the State House grounds, he could see a glimpse of the brick wall he'd been longing to see. His spirits lifting, he cut across the grounds and ran faster, trying not to trip on the endless trail of rubble. A few minutes later he was standing at the door of his ivy-covered home.

The door was locked, and he quickly rapped on it three times. A deep silence followed. He then forcefully rang the bell, delirious excitement taking over him. A few moments later there came the quick pattering of feet along the hall and the distant crying of a baby. Sallie opened the door and flew into his arms.

"Father!"

Mary Ann and Henry hurried up from the basement, Bessie came out from the kitchen with Carrie in her arms, and Emma, newly awakened, rushed down the stairs in disbelief. Within seconds the sisters were both hanging around Joseph's neck, their laughter mingling with tears. Joseph grabbed Carrie from Bessie's outstretched arms and placed excited kisses all over her face as Sallie and Emma pulled him inside the house.

EPILOGUE

AFTER THE WAR THE LECONTE family splintered. Emma married Confederate veteran Farish Furman and moved to a large plantation in central Georgia. Joseph and John (who returned to Columbia ten days later) both moved their families to Berkeley, California, where they were offered positions at the new University of California. Emma always longed to move out West to be closer to her family—especially her father, about whom she once wrote, "My dear father was always the center of my life." Joseph died in 1901 after a long and celebrated career.

Farish died of malaria in 1883, and Emma took over the running of the plantation and the education of her four daughters. She went on to live in Macon with her daughter Bess, at whose urging she wrote a second war diary, this one covering her experiences during World War I. She worked for the Red Cross, participated in the campaign to give women the right to vote, and later ran a school for black children. She died in 1932.

Nothing more is known about Charles Davis. He appears to have left Columbia without a trace. In their diaries both Joseph and Emma are confounded by his presence in their lives. Indeed, in his journal, Joseph writes of Davis, "Is he a Yankee spy? Or is he a spy on both sides? He is a greater mystery than ever."

Reverend Porter and Lieutenant McQueen's connection didn't end after the Yankees' departure from Columbia; the story of Porter's journey to free McQueen from Confederate captivity could fill another book. McQueen was wounded in a skirmish near Darlington ten days after the burning of Columbia, and he presented the letter that Reverend Porter had given him to a Confederate soldier who happened to know Porter. Reverend Porter, who had left Columbia and was camping in Anderson with his family, heard about McQueen's injury from a friend at the campsite. The friend warned Reverend Porter that there were some soldiers who believed the letter to be a forgery and McQueen to be an imposter. The reverend decided he had to try to find him. He traveled to Camden and tracked McQueen down to a hospital room where a dozen sick and wounded soldiers lay on the floor. Only one was dressed in blue. Porter had found him. He borrowed a buggy, and then he and McQueen headed north toward Virginia, where Porter was sure he could negotiate McQueen's safe transfer across enemy lines. Unable to get any farther than Raleigh, North Carolina, the men stopped, and Reverend Porter called on General Johnston, who arranged for McQueen to pass over to Sherman. The two men parted and never met again.

Columbia rebounded after the war, though South Carolina had years of economic, social, and political upheaval ahead of it. White elites, whose plantation system had brought them vast wealth, were now uncertain about their futures and were clashing with the large population of freed slaves who were striving to improve their economic and political circumstances. Federal troops would withdraw from the state in 1877, allowing white conservatives to take control of the state government once again. The economy suffered in the last decades of the nineteenth century, and it did not turn around until the first decade of the twentieth, when Columbia emerged as a major textile center. Other manufacturers soon moved into the state, bringing jobs and economic stability.

Today tourists can retrace Sherman's path through the city and walk among buildings—or what remains of them—that survived the fire of 1865.

AUTHOR'S NOTE

IN TRYING TO DEPICT AN event as devastating as the burning of Columbia, I faced a difficult task. Not only was this a chaotic episode involving the rapid destruction of the city, it was also one that, once the smoke had cleared, left a lot of questions that historians and Civil War buffs continue to debate today. Chief among these was whether it was Sherman's intention for his soldiers to burn the city, or if, rather, the "ocean of fire" was more the end result of a string of unfortunate coincidences—cotton stacked in the streets, soldiers given too much whiskey, and a forceful wind that allowed the flames to spread quickly. The general consensus among historians is that the fire was not deliberate, though there are still people who believe Sherman was intent on complete destruction of the city.

I was fortunate to be able to reference diaries, journals, and personal accounts that have been preserved for posterity. I relied heavily on the moving, haunting, and tragic first-person accounts of Emma LeConte, Joseph LeConte, and the Reverend Anthony Toomer Porter, not only in putting together the stories told in *Ocean of Fire* but also in understanding and empathizing with the people who committed their experiences to paper.

That said, it is an unfortunate truth that there are precious few slave accounts of this event in Columbia's history. Although Emma's diary does include passages about the house slaves, Henry and Mary Ann, we have nothing from the individuals themselves. Therefore, in order to get into the minds of these important characters, I needed to imagine what their lives were like and how their experience of the inferno and the incursion of Yankee soldiers was different from that of white Columbians. This was also true of Charles, the leader of the Niter Bureau slaves, and Sandy, John LeConte's slave, both of whom traveled with the LeConte brothers. They appeared in Joseph's journal, though his depiction of them is colored by his own fear and paranoia over their intentions toward him. In order to present them as independent bodies with their own motivations outside of Joseph's head, I had to rely upon conjecture and imagination.

I also needed to flesh out the character of Charles Davis, who appears in both Emma LeConte's and Joseph LeConte's accounts. Both Emma and Joseph find Mr. Davis a curious and somewhat mystifying presence, and neither of them fully trusts him. However, a full accounting of his actions during the burning of Columbia was never given. He himself left no journal or written document of his actions, so the two LeConte accounts are the only ones in the historical record. In order to round Mr. Davis out as a character during scenes when he was not in either of the LeConte homes, I had to imagine scenes that he could have played a part in, such as the shooting of the Yankee soldier and the burying of the explosives by the riverbank. Perhaps he did do these things. Perhaps he was a Yankee spy, perhaps a Confederate spy, or perhaps he was a double agent—we will never know for sure.

Photo Credits

ALSO IN THE HORRORS OF HISTORY SERIES

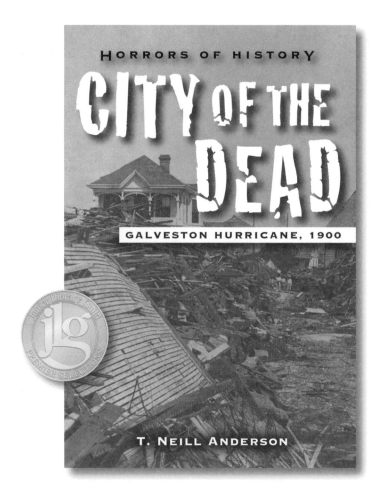

HORRORS OF HISTORY

CITY OF THE DEAD

GALVESTON HURRICANE, 1900

T. NEILL ANDERSON